Instructional Leadership

Instructional Leadership

Knowledge and Skills
for K–12 Success

Edited by
Frank S. Del Favero

ROWMAN & LITTLEFIELD
Lanham • Boulder • New York • London

Published by Rowman & Littlefield
An imprint of The Rowman & Littlefield Publishing Group, Inc.
4501 Forbes Boulevard, Suite 200, Lanham, Maryland 20706
www.rowman.com

6 Tinworth Street, London SE11 5AL, United Kingdom

British Library Cataloguing in Publication Information Available

Library of Congress Cataloging-in-Publication Data Is Available
ISBN 978-1-4758-3908-1 (cloth: alk. paper)
ISBN 978-1-4758-3909-8 (pbk: alk. paper)
ISBN 978-1-4758-3910-4 (electronic)

♾™ The paper used in this publication meets the minimum requirements of American National Standard for Information Sciences—Permanence of Paper for Printed Library Materials, ANSI/NISO Z39.48-1992.

Printed in the United States of America

I dedicate this book to all building-level leaders and teachers who undauntingly face the daily challenges and responsibilities of educating our youth. You do this while attempting to address learning standards and accountability measures, often with inadequate financial support. It is only through your professionalism, dedication, and sacrifice that your students have an opportunity to succeed!

Contents

Acknowledgments

This book could not have been possible without the presence of a strong spirit of cooperation, collaboration, and professionalism that exists among the faculty members of our Educational Foundations and Leadership department here at the University of Louisiana at Lafayette. Our faculty's abilities and experience as both researchers and practitioners significantly contributed to the value of this book, which serves as a reference for current school leaders and as an informational text for aspiring educational leaders.

I would like to specially thank our department head, Dr. Robert Slater, for his valuable help and inspiration as I planned, organized, and wrote chapters for this book. Maggi Bienvenu, one of our graduate assistants, also deserves special recognition for her work making certain that the chapters of this book follow the writing standards of the Chicago Manual of Style.

Introduction

Of the many challenges that all K–12 principals face today, it seems that one of the most pressing is the issue of accountability regarding student academic performance. State and federal initiatives seem to be the driving force that is mandating major changes in the way that we educate and assess our students. In addition to standardized test performance scores, educators, policymakers, and the general public are questioning and examining other K–12 educational quality and performance measures such as graduation rates, attendance, student discipline infractions, dropout percentages, teacher quality, student enrollment stability, teacher retention rates, and high school graduates' activities such as acceptance, enrollment, and graduation rates at two- and four-year postsecondary institutions, entrance into the workforce, military, etc.

In fact, even without the existence of state and federal mandates, an effective school leader still needs to address these educational quality and performance measures in order to provide students with high-quality educational experiences that will prepare them to be effective lifelong learners who will become contributing members to society able to compete successfully on the world stage. Achieving this goal is a complex and difficult challenge that requires educational leaders to possess extensive knowledge and skills in the areas of instruction and organizational development.

Currently, K–12 principals recognize the need to improve their respective schools. Unfortunately, many of them have not had the opportunity to develop and refine the requisite knowledge and skills to affect positive school change. The goal of *Instructional Leadership: Knowledge and Skills for K–12 Success* is to provide K–12 practitioners as well as aspiring educational leaders with the knowledge and skills needed to affect instructional success in the areas of data analysis, evaluation of instruction and assessment, and organizing and leading a school. *Instructional Leadership: Knowledge and Skills for K–12*

Success can be a valuable resource for both practitioners and aspiring educational leaders who are avidly searching for meaningful and detailed information to initiate instructional success in a K–12 environment.

PURPOSE

The purpose of this publication is to guide a school-building-level administrator or aspiring educational leader through the process of developing appropriate instructional knowledge and skills needed to affect change that will lead to success. This text will help the building-level administrator become a more effective educational leader. It will suggest how she can develop and share her instructional knowledge and skills with the school's faculty in a manner that will create a strong sense of community and collaboration that is focused on improving student academic performance. Essentially, the purpose of this book is to provide educational leaders with what they need to know regarding instruction, the integration and implementation of which will lead to significant progress and success in addressing the challenges involved in school improvement.

WHO WILL USE *INSTRUCTIONAL LEADERSHIP: KNOWLEDGE AND SKILLS FOR K–12 SUCCESS?*

Instructional Leadership: Knowledge and Skills for K–12 Success is meant to serve a variety of users that includes but is not limited to central office personnel, school board members, parents, community members, building-level administrators, and faculty members. At the district level, *Instructional Leadership: Knowledge and Skills for K–12 Success* can serve as a concise, sequentially organized reference text for central office administrators (superintendents, subject area specialists, supervisors, etc.). The book could also be used to initiate and guide professional development in the area of school improvement for building principals, team members, and any additional central office and building-level staff responsible for instruction.

EDITOR'S NOTE

Instructional Leadership: Knowledge and Skills for K–12 Success and its companion *Organizational Leadership: Knowledge and Skills for K–12*

Success are the product of collaboration among the faculty of the Master of Educational Leadership degree program at the University of Louisiana at Lafayette, College of Education, Department of Educational Foundations and Leadership.

Chapter 1

The Many Facets of School Data

Frank S. Del Favero, PhD

THE IMPORTANT ROLE DATA PLAYS IN OUR LIVES

We live in a data-driven world. Data plays important roles in industries such as manufacturing and entertainment, and in service industries such as healthcare, marketing, and insurance, to mention a few. No one can deny the important role that data has played and will continue to play in political campaigns where it is used to collect voters' perceptions of political and policy issues and voter demographics such as race, gender, age, level of education, occupation, level of income, political party affiliation, where voters live and work, etc., to construct and refine campaign strategies that will satisfy and attract voters and financial contributors.

Insurance companies use data to predict life expectancies based on gender, age, occupation, and health to determine the costs of premiums. Retailers use data as an integral part of their product inventory and ordering process. Wholesalers and retailers routinely use trend data showing past sales and customer demographics, among a plethora of other data types and sources, to determine pricing and inventory size.

With respect to data, processes common among all industries and organizations that routinely use data involve the following:

1. Collection of a variety of data types
2. Careful and accurate analysis of data to inform strategy and policy-making decisions that impact the future direction of an organization
3. Continuous evaluation of inputs and outputs
4. Analysis of input and output data as part of the problem-solving process
5. Routine application of the Root Cause Analysis (RCA) process

On a more personal level, we regularly use measures of various data types over time. An example that comes to mind to illustrate this point is the family car. When we plan a road trip, we determine such things as the destination, the distance of the destination, the cost of fuel, the duration of the trip, the number and cost of meals, and overnight stays. We analyze these data to help us determine whether we can afford the predicted costs.

If the costs are more than expected, we use the data to inform our decision and perhaps choose another, less costly destination. Even before we start our road trip, we rely on our automobiles to provide us with an assortment of necessary data such as tire pressure, oil, coolant, fuel levels, and the condition of the battery to address the automotive systems that may be identified as needing attention. Most of our vehicles will inform us of the average mile per gallon rate. This information will help us determine where and how many times we will need to stop to refuel.

Once we enter our destination data into our GPS device, we receive and use the data it provides to guide our trip. It is obvious to this writer and will presumably be to you, the reader, that data play an integral and important role at both the societal and personal levels. The gathering and accurate analysis of data are essential steps to success at both levels. As educators, we must ask ourselves if we efficiently and effectively use data in the same manner as we use them in our industries and at the personal level.

OUTPUT AND INPUT DATA

It has been this writer's experience that many K–12 schools do routinely use data. Unfortunately, most educational organizations focus almost all of their attention on student performance data, which include student grades from locally developed formative and summative assessments and from standardized tests developed at the national and/or state levels. They also look at high school graduation and school dropout rates. One could characterize these data sources as *output data*.

Output data is limited in that it can only identify a state or condition. *Output data* cannot inform us why or how we arrived at a particular state or condition. If we know the WHY and the HOW (*input data*), we can accurately identify the area(s) of concern and address the issues. Let us return to our knowledge of automobiles to illustrate this concept. We can begin by comparing the gasoline mileage of two identical cars. The *output data* of car A is thirty miles per gallon of fuel. The *output data* of car B indicates that it uses one gallon of fuel to go thirty-four miles. Since these cars are identical, we have to assume that there must be other factors (*input data*) that influence these numbers such as the:

1. driving habits of the driver of each vehicle,
2. condition of the tires and the tire pressure,
3. weather (temperature, wind speed, and precipitation),
4. condition of the engines and roads, and
5. quality of fuel.

Based on the example above, it is easy to see that additional factors represented as *input data* play an important role in influencing fuel economy *output data*. An auto mechanic's analysis of these *input data* will find the root cause(s) of the discrepancy in mileage rates between the two identical cars and appropriately address the identified problem(s), resulting in the probable improvement of the mileage rate of at least car A and possibly car B as well.

Unfortunately, many K–12 organizations ignore many of the other data types that are readily available in schools. It is relatively easy to understand why this is the case. Lawmakers, policymakers, and the general public hold public schools in general and teachers and administrators specifically accountable for public school performance as measured by standardized test scores. Since state and national accountability measures of an organization's level of success examine primarily *output data* of student academic performance, which is represented by standardized test scores, most K–12 organizations limit their analysis of data to student achievement scores on standardized tests. To summarize, an analysis of *output data* can only indicate the state or condition of academic performance. A school's failure to collect and analyze *input data* to determine the WHY and HOW of student academic performance scores will doom school change and improvement efforts.

THE FOUR SCHOOL DATA TYPES

It is important to note that there are a variety of data types, most of which can be characterized as *input data*. In no particular order, the first data type is classified as (1) *school academic performance data*. Academic performance data is probably the most widely recognized data type. This data type measures academic performance on all kinds of formative and summative of assessments. (2) *Demographic data* deals with information regarding the social and economic status, gender, race, ethnicity, language spoken in the home, and education level of all stakeholders in a school community. (3) *Perception data* is probably the most overlooked and misunderstood of the four data types. Perception data represents the stakeholders' general beliefs regarding the state of the school. The fourth and final data type is (4) *school process data*. This data type represents the processes that support teaching and learning. It is established and implemented so that the school can function efficiently and effectively.

A careful collection and analysis of input and output data provided by each of the four data types is a critical step in the school improvement process. The analysis of each of the data types will identify areas of success as well as areas that need attention. An organization can determine the extent that improvement strategies impact teaching and learning by examining areas of success and areas of concern. The analysis will provide a school organization with information regarding strategies and interventions that are working, strategies that are working but require slight modifications, and strategies that are not working at all and that we can abandon.

Before one can delve into the collection and analysis of the four data types, one must have a good understanding of the composition of each of the data types. In the following paragraphs, it is hoped that the reader will gain a comprehensive understanding of each of the four data types.

SCHOOL ACADEMIC PERFORMANCE

School academic performance data consists of assessment data. Assessment data can be *informal*. Informal assessment data are data that are not recorded (as opposed to formal assessments whose results are recorded) and are usually part of a teacher's *formative* assessment strategies. Formative assessment is generally defined as assessments that are made during the instructional process (i.e., while students are constructing or "forming" new knowledge). Informal formative assessments, a strategy commonly known as "checking for understanding," are administered during the instructional process. This type of assessment informs both the teacher and the learner.

The teacher discovers the depth and extent of student learning based on student responses to teacher-generated oral questions during the presentation of a lesson. The teacher uses the student responses to inform her decision on whether to continue progressing through the material or to revise, modify, and repeat the presentation of the material. It is also important to note that teachers should consider using informal formative assessment results to help them set realistic classroom-level academic goals.

Students are informed regarding the status and effectiveness of their own learning when they compare the responses of their colleagues with their own responses. The responses of classmates as well as their own help the students realize whether they are understanding and learning the ideas and concepts being presented. This information helps them to decide whether to ask a question seeking further clarification, to pay stricter attention during the lessons, or to increase their level of participation in the learning activities.

Formal formative assessments typically include quizzes, unit tests, research papers, performance tasks, and benchmark assessments, and recorded grades.

Formative assessments provide educators with *input data*. These data represent the results of the efforts made by teachers and administrators to improve academic performance. Formal formative assessments provide student performance data, which are gathered during the teaching and learning process throughout the school year. Specifically, formative assessment data can be used to judge the state of teaching and learning during the school year.

Through continuous evaluation and analysis of formative assessment data, teachers and administrators are able to monitor the effectiveness of teaching strategies and school improvement plans. Teachers and administrators can use this knowledge to make ongoing modifications and adjustments to teaching and school improvement strategies that are designed to address identified areas of concern.

Summative assessments, on the other hand, measure academic performance based on assessments that are administered at the very end of the school year. Summative assessments include standardized tests and teacher- or state-generated End of Course (EOC) examinations. These *output data* are a product of the educational interventions that were introduced, monitored, and modified as necessary during the school year.

It is necessary to note here that although some school organizations place all of their focus and efforts on academic scores, schools are not one-dimensional organizations. There are other factors present that interact with each other and have an impact on the overall health and effectiveness of the institution. These other factors are represented by additional types of *input data*. The next data type we will discuss is *demographic data*.

DEMOGRAPHIC DATA

Demographic data provides useful information regarding stakeholders in the school community. If routinely and accurately gathered and analyzed, this data provides school officials with information about such things as ethnicity, socioeconomic status, level of education, educational classification, age, gender, marital status, employment status, family size, housing status, residential address, phone numbers, and language(s) spoken at home. It should be noted here that demographic data is not limited to only the students/clients the school serves. Demographic data should paint an accurate picture of all stakeholders living and working within the school community, including information on all residents (whether they have children attending school or not) and all school district employees assigned to the school.

The reader might wonder why it is necessary to collect and analyze demographic data of the entire school community in addition to the obvious demographic data relating to the students themselves. In the following sections, this writer describes the reasons for and purpose of gathering demographic data, which represent the demographic makeup of the entire school as well as of the people who live and work in the community that it serves.

Student Demographic Data

Educators use student demographic data in a variety of ways—for example, to determine the number and size of classes in each grade level in an elementary school. At the middle- and high-school levels, administrators use demographic data to determine the number of sections for each course. Knowing the numbers of needed classes and sections will help to determine the number of instructional staff members the school would need to serve its students effectively.

Data relating to the students' native language helps educators determine the need and extent to provide English as a Second Language (ESL) support. Rather than examining student academic performance data as a whole, where the results provide little, if any, useful information regarding the effects of implementation of school improvement strategies, the disaggregation of student academic performance data based on student demographic data can provide more comprehensive information about academic performance.

The concepts *equity* and *social justice* play very important roles in education. Disaggregating academic performance data by gender and ethnicity can reveal the extent that the school addresses all students' academic needs in an equitable manner. Disaggregating the student academic performance data even further by, for example, Socioeconomic Status (SES) and educational classification (student exceptionalities such as special education, 504, and/or gifted and talented) will reveal additional detailed information that could be used to discover and address academic performance gaps based on, for example, gender, SES, ethnicity, and educational classification. In this manner, educators are able to identify student groups that may or may not be performing at acceptable levels. These are but a few examples of how educators can use student demographic data to measure and assess school efficiencies as well as the extent that educational programs are equitable. The characteristics of the school's instructional and noninstructional staff are just as important as those of students and other stakeholders.

Teacher Demographic Data

School administrators need to be fully aware of the abilities and limitations of their teaching personnel so that they can effectively use their staff by making appropriate teaching assignments. School leaders use teacher demographic data to identify potential leaders, effective teachers, as well as teachers who may need assistance in further developing and refining their instructional skills. Teacher demographic data can also assist them as it provides and supports their instructional staff with meaningful continuing education/professional development opportunities. During this era of accountability, the collection and analysis of teacher demographic data is therefore critically important to the ability of a school to produce emotionally and academically successful students.

An accurate and comprehensive database of teacher demographics should contain information such as contact information, gender, work and educational histories, teaching certifications, years teaching in each certification area, measures of teacher performance as represented by formal evaluations, and professional development/continuing education experiences. Just as in the case of student demographic and academic performance data, administrators can disaggregate teacher demographic data with academic performance data to identify teachers whose students achieve higher academic performance scores as well as those teachers who may not be as effective. Comparing the academic scores earned by the students of various teachers with the teachers' participation in professional development can yield information regarding the effectiveness of past and/or ongoing professional development programs. These are just a few examples of how educational leaders can use teacher demographic data as part of the school improvement process.

Although student and teacher demographic data make up a considerable portion of demographic data relating to a school organization, one cannot ignore the importance of knowing and understanding the demographics of the people who live within the school community.

School Community Demographics

School community demographics include the demographic information of the parents whose children are currently enrolled in the school and of the general population of the community who do not have direct ties to the school. Specifically, the general population consists of businesses and individuals who are not employees of the school, and do not have children attending school. Demographic information relating to this demographic category includes, but is not limited to, residential and business addresses, employment status, education level, whether the individual owns or rents, income level, language(s) spoken in the home, age, and gender.

School officials can use demographic data in a variety of ways. Knowing the number and age of the children living within the school's geographic boundaries are critical elements in predicting future school populations. Educators can use these data to inform decisions regarding future staffing, class size, and possible future school construction and renovation projects.

School administrators can use these demographic data to examine and predict employment trends, which can be a reliable indicator of future population growth or decline. Employment trends are effective predictors of economic trends at both the state and local levels. School boards and district-level administration use these data to set tax rates and construct school district budgets.

It is important to mention here that this writer used demographic data relating to the education level of students' mothers to predict and identify which students were likely to drop out of school before graduation. Researchers have discovered that the mother's level of education has a statistically significant correlation that predicts the child's level of education.

With this in mind, the writer analyzed the student registration data and created a list identifying students whose mothers failed to earn a high school diploma. *(In this writer's school alone, 16 percent of our students' mothers had not earned a high school diploma.)* This list was shared with the students' respective principals and guidance counselors, who monitored the students' progress and provided necessary interventions as they progressed through the grades. Although one cannot measure negatives, one can safely assume that these actions had an impact on the district's dropout rate.

PERCEPTION DATA

Unfortunately, perception data are overlooked, often receiving little if any attention by members of school improvement teams, faculty, and administrators. What educators see and perceive represents their "reality." They fail to consider the thoughts, beliefs, and perceptions of the clients (students, parents, and the community) they serve. Educational leaders must understand and realize that perceptions drive the actions of the faculty, staff, students, parents, and other stakeholders. Their actions are based on what they believe to be their reality.

There are three general methods that one uses to gather and ultimately analyze perception data. The first method is through surveys involving closed responses. Survey questions requiring closed responses can involve a question followed by multiple choice responses, where the participant chooses one or more answers from two or more choices. A second type of closed response survey requires the participant to read a statement or question and to select a response on a scale indicating various levels of degrees of agreement or dis-agreement. The third type of survey question requires the respondent to write out his/her response.

Awareness of the perceptions of the clients one serves is a crucial step in the school change process. The challenge for educators is to change the perceptions of the people they serve as well as their own if necessary.

Student Perception Data

As an example, let us assume that students are complaining about instances of bullying. In order to learn more about this situation, you decide to create and administer a short survey to the students in your sixth, seventh, and eighth grade middle school. Your survey questions provide you with information on where and when bullying instances occur. You also have been able to determine the number, gender, and ethnicity of students at each grade level who observe or are targets themselves of bullying as well as the same information regarding the student(s) acting as bullies. Your analysis of these data indicate that bullying occurs, for the most part, among the seventh and eighth grade boys who participate in athletics and that the instances of bullying generally occur in the locker room before and after daily practice.

The principal can share this information with the appropriate coaches and work with them to establish or refine policies regarding bullying. They can also devise plans to improve supervision in the locker rooms and lessen the chances for bullying to occur. In addition, a schoolwide campaign against bullying can be initiated. Future surveys of student perceptions of student bullying can be used to determine if the new policies and interventions have had a positive impact on the bullying situation.

The example above demonstrates the important but often overlooked role that perception data can play in identifying and solving problems that are not necessarily academic in nature but whose solutions can have a positive influence on academics. Students who feel safe and secure are more likely to be active participants in the teaching and learning process.

Teacher Perception Data

An effective school leader knows that the perceptions of the instructional and noninstructional staff are both instrumental in the proper functioning of the school organization. The beliefs held by the school's staff impact school climate and culture, which in turn can determine, for example, the level of success or failure of school improvement plans and change initiatives. Teacher perception surveys can be very informative and address a wide variety of beliefs regarding, but not limited to, expectations of academic performance of all students regardless of ethnicity or gender, and of the principal's leadership characteristics and his ability to lead.

More specifically, information gleaned from teacher perceptions, for example, of the extent they (1) can trust the principal, (2) have confidence in the principal's ability to fairly and consistently observe and evaluate teacher classroom performance, (3) believe that the principal supports the teaching staff, (4) believe the principal has high expectations of all students and staff, (5) believe the principal has good communication skills, and (6) believe that the principal has extensive knowledge and skills in a wide range of instructional and assessment strategies, can be very useful. These are but a few examples of the topics that can be addressed in a teacher perception survey and the answers to which can serve to identify perceived strengths and weaknesses in the principal's leadership qualities, instructional programs, etc. The principal, armed with teacher perception data, can use survey data to identify areas of concern and begin interventions to affect change.

Parent Perception Data

The same can be stated of parent perception data that has been said about student and teacher perception data. It is important to know how parents feel about the schools their children attend. What they feel is their reality and it is the responsibility of the school to work with the parents and to take whatever steps are necessary to change their perceptions. Please note that these changes may involve improving the frequency and quality of communication between the school and home, or actual changes to school policies and processes.

School personnel can use parental perception data to discover concerns and possibly misconceptions parents may have regarding the functioning of the school. For example, perception surveys of parents could be used to discover parents' thoughts regarding (1) home/school communication, (2) information regarding the curricula and assessments, (3) the quality of instruction, (4) the extent that teachers care for and support their students, (5) teacher expectations in the area of academic performance, and (6) school discipline, etc. Again, the questions in parent perception surveys, as they are in teacher and student surveys, are limited only by the personnel who create the survey questions.

SCHOOL PROCESS DATA

The fourth and final data type used in our schools deals with school processes. Process data come in a variety of forms and generally represent the various processes and systems that provide information on the day-to-day functioning of the school. The writer provides here several examples of school process data:

1. The master schedule provides information about when and where classes take place. It also indicates the names of the teachers and students assigned to each class section.
2. The student schedule provides individual students with the names of courses, teachers, and the location of each course they are assigned to take.
3. The school academic calendar contains information regarding the dates school is in session as well as the dates it is in recess. The calendar also contains information regarding any events that may have an impact on instruction such as teacher workshops and testing.
4. The teacher duty schedule lists the noninstructional duties, the times and locations for each duty, and the name the teacher assigned to each particular duty.
5. The student guidance folders contain historical information, in addition to academic records and any number and variety of records relating to a student's personal information such as psychological reports, minutes of meetings with staff and parents, a student's educational classification and supporting documents (regular education, special education, other health impaired [504], English language proficiency), demographic information, etc.
6. Student discipline data contain information regarding discipline referrals a student may have received, the author of the referral, the date, a description of the infraction, and the location where the infraction took place. The discipline data also include the consequence(s) or penalty administered, and the name of the adjudicator of the infraction.
7. The professional development data consist of records of the extent and content of any professional development in which a teacher has participated.
8. Teacher observation and evaluation data provide a running record of a classroom teacher's effectiveness and performance in the classroom.
9. Data relating to any particular or specialized instructional approaches routinely used in a content area include but are not limited to reading comprehension programs or programs that focus on developing student skills in solving complex math word problems.
10. Response to Intervention (RtI) data serve to keep track of students who were identified and diagnosed as academically needy. The data help to identify and implement a particular instructional intervention aimed at developing an identified student's knowledge and skills.

CHAPTER SUMMARY

In this chapter we have discussed the roles that data plays in our daily lives. We take for granted and routinely use data, for example the variety and range of data provided by our cars' fuel, pressure, temperature, odometer, speedometer gauge, and navigation system to provide us with the information we need when we travel in our cars. We have also discussed the fact that, unfortunately, many schools and school systems focus solely on student academic data to form the basis of school improvement strategies and interventions. This chapter has presented and discussed three additional types of data that are available to schools to inform decisions regarding school improvement and change efforts. Schools can also use the information gained from these additional data types to more clearly identify and define the factors that impact the functioning of the school and in turn impact academic performance.

The effective instructional leader realizes that academic performance, as well as demographic, perception, and school process data, represents most if not all of the factors that impact school efficiencies. She also knows that these factors are all interdependent and influence the outcomes of each other. A successful school leader understands that successful interventions and change efforts require careful analysis of the interactions of all four of the school data types to identify areas of success as well as areas needing attention. These findings are used to inform her and her school improvement team's decisions regarding the development and implementation of intervention strategies. The following chapter, which deals with root cause analysis, demonstrates how data analysis of multiple data types can be used to identify the root cause(s) of an area of concern.

Chapter 2

Data Analysis

Looking for the "Root Cause"

Frank S. Del Favero, PhD

The challenges that K–12 educators and school leaders face today are very complex, and the strategies that they use to address them are, more often than not, inadequate. They have little if any effect in overcoming these challenges. It is recognized that there are many factors that impact student learning and school processes. Educators are often able to identify areas of concern such as student discipline, academics, teacher retention, etc. They may "solve" the student discipline problem by revising the discipline code, attempting to raise academic performance by providing tutoring for at-risk students, or changing the length of class periods. The solutions tend to be one-dimensional and based on anecdotal and/or biased assumptions rather than on data-based information.

The purpose of this chapter is to present and discuss the concept of Root Cause Analysis (RCA) and how this process, which has its origins in the various fields of engineering as a troubleshooting tool, can be used in K–12 education. The chapter introduces examples of the application of RCA in noneducational settings so that the reader may gain a basic understanding of the process. The presenter will then introduce a brief case study of how student performance, as well as demographic, school process, and perception data, when used with the RCA process, can be applied in a school setting to effectively address problem areas.

The chapter will also discuss, examine, and demonstrate how to use root cause analysis to identify problem areas and provide some examples of research-based solutions to address these hypothetical problems. This chapter will show that multiple measures of various data sources over time will help in the development of a richer and more detailed "picture" of a school's performance and of the many variables that influence it. The chapter will show how to look for "trends" in the data, that is, measures of data taken over a period of time as opposed to isolated one-time "snapshots" of the state of the school organization as depicted through one-dimensional data models.

In the past many educators, intent on improving their students' academic performance, hastily sought out solutions that often superficially identified areas of concern as causes of poor academic achievement. The "solutions" were often based on anecdotal data and observations that were, for the most part, unscientific, inaccurate, incomplete, not thoroughly researched, and often influenced by the personal bias of the observer.

The actions and strategies that were chosen as solutions to the problem of poor academic performance could be characterized as inappropriate, poorly conceived, improperly implemented, untested, and unproven. School improvement processes as described above produced results that were often disappointing and discouraging because they appeared to be ineffectual. Following this process year after year, school leaders and instructional staff became increasingly frustrated due to the lack of measurable and consistent improvement.

The root cause analysis process, if applied properly, can ease frustrations and disappointments while affecting a significant positive impact on school improvement.

ROOT CAUSE ANALYSIS TO FIX A LEAKING PIPE

An analogy that one could use to help members of a School Leadership Team (SLT) and/or students participating in the school improvement process to develop a better grasp of the concept of root cause analysis follows:

The problem involves the discovery of a puddle of water on the basement floor. At the initial discovery of the water puddle, one would quickly mop up the water and hope that the problem had been addressed. A further check a few minutes later reveals that there is yet another puddle of water on the floor. The next quickest and easiest solution would be to place a bucket on the floor at the location of the puddle of water. The immediate result of this action is that there is no longer a growing and dangerous puddle of water on the floor. However, the bucket is slowly filling and will soon overflow onto the floor. There is no water on the floor now but there soon will be.

Since the problem persists, one is forced to begin the search for a cause or causes. The initial search reveals that there is only one puddle on the floor and that there are no cracks in the floor through which the water could seep. This finding rules out the need to repair the floor. However, one notices directly above the puddle on the floor a hot water pipe, a cold water pipe, and a waste water pipe. Now the next task is to determine which pipe(s) is/ are leaking. If the water puddle is warm, then one could safely assume that the hot water pipe is the source of the problem. If the water puddle is cold, then an assumption could be made that the cold water pipe is the source of problem. The same could be said of the waste water pipe, if the water puddle were made up of waste water. Note that we have not yet solved our problem.

Up to this point, we have only identified the problem and made an assumption as to the general source of the problem. *Remember that we are still looking for the root cause of the problem and for the most appropriate and effective method or methods to solve it.* In this example, let's assume that the water puddle contains warm water and therefore, the warm water pipe is the source of the problem. We know that water leaks can be caused by (1) a crack in the pipe that can be repaired by replacing the cracked section of pipe, (2) a loose connection that can be repaired by using a wrench to tighten the connection, or (3) a defective or worn valve or fitting that can be repaired by replacing the defective part or parts. In our case, a careful inspection of the hot water pipe reveals that the pipe has a crack in it. We replace the cracked section of pipe. We still need to determine what actually caused the pipe to crack.

Our further inspection of the pipe reveals that insulation was missing from the area on the pipe where the crack occurred. We then reason that during the recent cold spell, the missing insulation allowed the water in the pipe to freeze and expand, causing the pipe to split. We have now uncovered what we assume to be the root causes that created a puddle of water on our floor: (1) the crack in the hot water pipe and (2) the missing insulation that allowed the pipe to freeze and to crack. We've solved our problem—or have we?

It is both important and necessary to monitor the solutions to our problems. Upon further examination of our repairs the next morning, we discover a small puddle of water in the same location as the original puddle. Following the same procedures as discussed above, we determine that during our original repair of the hot water pipe, we failed to properly tighten one of the fittings. After making the appropriate repair, we continue to monitor the area below the repair as well as all of the other pipes in the basement, searching for evidence that further interventions may be required. After further monitoring, no additional leaks are found and no additional interventions are necessary. All is well—problem solved! If only school improvement were this easy and straightforward!

MULTIPLE MEASURES OF DATA

In her book, *Data Analysis for Continuous School Improvement* (second edition, 2004), Victoria Bernhardt addresses some interesting and important concepts regarding data analysis. According to Bernhardt, effective data analysis involves multiple measures of data over time. As part of the school improvement process, an accurate and meaningful analysis of data is critical to the success of any school improvement interventions.

Our pipe repair analogy clearly parallels the Root Cause Analysis process in that it involves the analysis of multiple measures of data (the puddle of water on the floor, the cracked pipe, the missing insulation, the recent cold snap, the loose fitting, and our regular monitoring of all of these variables after the interventions were initiated). In most typical educational settings, one can find several types of data that include but are not limited to

1. demographic data relating to the students, their parents, the community, as well as the school's instructional and noninstructional staff;
2. student academic performance data, which include standardized test scores, report card data, dropout and graduation rates, and diagnostic assessments, to name a few;
3. school process data that provides information on how a school functions, such as the school master schedule, student discipline data, student and faculty attendance rates, teacher training (professional development), class size, etc.; and
4. perception data representing what parents, students, teachers, and community members believe to be true regarding teaching and learning.

Unfortunately, many school improvement efforts target solely student academic performance data, ignoring, for example, student demographic data such as gender, ethnicity, education classification (special education, 504, gifted and talented), school process, and perception data. Uncovering if and where these data types intersect is the key to identifying the root cause and implementing strategies that address it. Intersections of data types often provide insight and point to the root cause.

For example, student performance data on statewide assessments may intersect with demographic data that suggest that African-American males perform significantly lower than their white counterparts. An examination of school process data involving discipline—specifically, out of school suspension rates—may indicate that African-American males are suspended out of school at higher rates than white males. In this hypothetical case, the root cause may lie in the school discipline process, classroom management, and the instructional approaches or strategies applied in the classroom that may not adequately address the educational needs of African-American male students.

Not to be ignored, an examination of these same intersections over time helps to distinguish a long-term trend from a temporary up- or downturn in student performance. Examining multiple data types over time is an effective approach in identifying the target of the interventions (in this hypothetical case, African-American males with high out-of-school suspension rates). This approach will also effectively help to uncover the root cause and possible intervention strategies that can have a positive impact on the target student population's academic performance.

ROOT CAUSE ANALYSIS FOR COST-EFFICIENT AND EFFECTIVE PROBLEM-SOLVING

One might assume that school improvement interventions and strategies involve costly professional development initiatives and/or investments in the acquisition of new textbook series. Fortunately, this is not the case in many instances. The short scenario that follows is an example:

Bill Farmer, an experienced and recently retired school principal, was hired in December as an interim principal to temporarily replace the principal of a suburban high school with a ninth–twelfth-grade population of 634 students who was fired that November by the school superintendent and board of education. Wanting to avoid last-minute surprises and disappointments among seniors and their parents as they approached graduation in June, in December Bill asked his guidance counselors to prepare a list of seniors who might be in danger of not graduating because of poor grades in English 4 and social studies 4. It is important to note that in Bill's state, among other requirements, students must earn at least 4 credits in English and social studies in order to earn a high school diploma.

In the past, Bill routinely used a "Seniors Who Are At Risk" list to arrange face-to-face meetings with each at-risk senior and his/her parents. At the meetings, he reminded them of the seriousness of their situation, specifically, that they would not be able to graduate in June if they did not work to improve their grades. Throughout the remainder of the school year Bill had the list regularly updated and stayed in contact with the identified seniors. In his previous positions, these interventions served as an effective "wake-up call," and fortunately most of the students eventually worked their way off the "Seniors Who Are At Risk" list.

It was a bit different in Bill's current job. As the school year progressed, Bill found that the constant monitoring and meetings were taking up a great deal of his time. He decided to begin to look for reasons why many of his seniors were appearing on his at-risk list. His first step involved looking at the report card grades of his failing seniors. While he examined the report card grades, he noticed that many of his identified seniors had high rates of tardiness to school.

He found this unusual and began to problem-solve. Since over 80 percent of the students in the school either drove or rode busses to school, he decided to check with the transportation supervisor. He learned that the busses were rarely late in the mornings and students were routinely delivered to school on time. He next checked with the school crossing guard to learn whether students who drove to school were arriving late. The crossing guard who was stationed in front of the school said that very rarely did students arrive late to school. He did note, however, that parents drove most of the cars that were late. With this information, Bill was able to rule out school transportation or students driving to school as a reason for the tardiness.

He next looked at the class schedules of the identified at-risk seniors and almost immediately discovered that the first class on many of their schedules was either English 4 or social studies 4. An examination of student referrals received by at-risk seniors revealed an unusually high number of referrals for late arrivals to first period classes. With the results of his preliminary data analysis in hand, he began to think that he was homing in on the cause of the problem.

Bill next used the teacher assignment schedule to identify English 4 and social studies 4 teachers who had first period class assignments. He questioned these teachers and confirmed the fact that many of the at-risk seniors often missed the first 10 to 15 minutes of class. Bill also learned that they caused disruptions to both teaching and learning because of their late arrivals to class.

For the next step in his investigation, Bill decided to speak to some of his at-risk seniors. During his discussions with them, he discovered that many of the seniors who drove to school remained in their cars beyond the start of school bell, socializing, listening to music, or doing "other things that were not related to learning." He also learned that many of the seniors who rode busses to school, rather than going into the building from the busses, joined their friends in their cars in the parking lot.

Bill next examined the teacher duty assignment schedule. He discovered that no one was assigned to supervise the student parking lot in the morning before classes. The principal realized that he needed someone to supervise the school parking lot who would make certain that students would leave their cars and enter the building as soon as they arrived in the parking lot. He was not able to immediately assign teachers to supervise the student parking lot because the teachers' contract with the school district did not allow for teaching or supervisory duty assignments either before the beginning or after the end of the contractual day.

Bill's challenge was to find a way around this dilemma. Based on his conversations with some of the younger teachers, Bill knew that many of the younger teaching staff members had to pick up their children from preschools or babysitters at the end of the school day. After checking with teacher association representatives, his solution was to approach these teachers and ask them if they would be willing to begin their teaching day fifteen minutes earlier than what was stated in the contract. In exchange, he would allow them to leave school fifteen minutes earlier at the end of the school day so that they could get an earlier start picking up their children at the end of the day.

Two teachers gladly accepted this arrangement and began to supervise the student parking lot the next day. Soon, there was a significant drop in referrals for tardiness to first period classes. The numbers of students on the at-risk seniors list also began to show a significant decrease in numbers. It is important to note that Bill's solution to the problem was accomplished in a manner that did not involve additional financial expenditures on the part of the school district and had little if any impact on school processes.

While not all of the challenges school principals face are as easy to solve or as quickly solved as the one presented in this case study, the writer believes this case study serves as a good example that illustrates the RCA process. The benefits of RCA are extensive in that it provides school improvement teams with a rich and meaningful assortment of data that can be used to create and implement effective and measurable intervention strategies that serve to lessen or eliminate altogether any issues that impede student learning.

This case study also serves to show that an effective analysis of data is not limited to student performance data; it includes several other types of data such as school process data that includes, but is not limited to, discipline referrals, teacher assignment schedules, and student schedules. The process also looks at, in this case, both student and teacher demographic data. Please note that Bill's RCA focused on data intersections (where two or more data types and/or sources intersect) to help him to narrow down the range of possible causes.

In the past, principals facing similar situations might have followed their "gut feelings" and "knee-jerk reactions" to create intervention strategies that typically involved assigning after-school tutoring sessions for the identified students on the "Seniors Who Are At Risk" list. This case study illustrates that a tutoring program (one of the more common intervention strategies used in schools today to address academic performance issues) would not have solved the identified problem as well as the solution that Bill employed.

The flowchart below illustrates the process the principal followed to discover the root cause of failing grades earned by seniors in English language arts (ELA) classes. He discovered the root cause by (1) using demographic data to identify the seniors, (2) examining report card ELA grades to determine at-risk seniors, (3) using school process data to discover that many of the identified students had high instances of tardiness, (4) using school

Frank S. Del Favero, PhD

Root Cause Analysis Flowchart for Case Study:

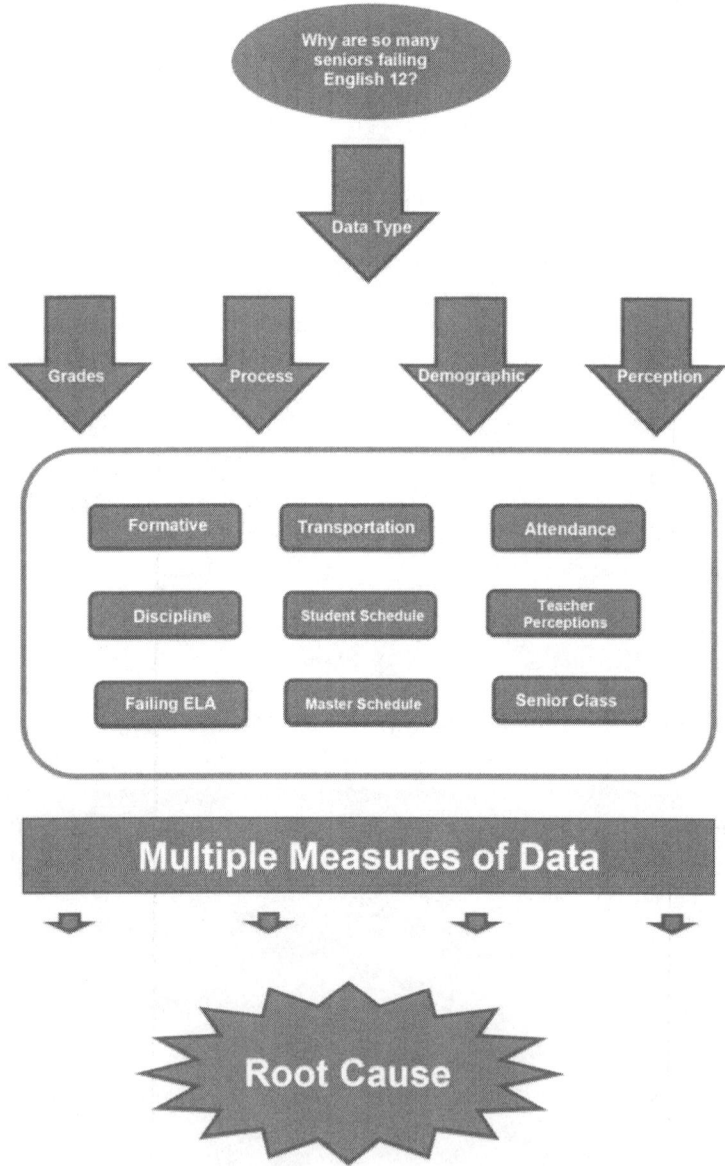

Figure 2.1.

process data (in this case, student schedules) to discover that many of the identified seniors were scheduled in first period ELA classes, (5) using school process data (transportation and attendance) to determine the arrival times of busses and instances of tardiness, and (6) using school process data (teacher duty schedules which are part of the school's master schedule) to determine teacher bus duty assignments and speaking with the assigned teachers regarding their perceptions of the problem. He learned that many students were remaining in their cars instead of entering the building as soon as they arrived. The principal realized that students were taking advantage of the fact that no one was assigned to supervise the student parking lot, resulting in tardiness to first period classes.

CHAPTER SUMMARY

In this chapter we have learned that schools could greatly benefit by adopting the RCA process routinely used in industry and other private sector organizations to diagnose and identify the factors and their interactions that result in problems that impinge on the efficient functioning of an organization. Leaders in the private sector realize that factors that contribute to the creation of problems are not simple and one-dimensional.

They know, for example, that in order to determine the cause of a downward trend in revenue from sales, they need to look beyond sales data. The RCA process requires an examination of all the factors that may impact sales (quality control, advertising, product quality, buyer perceptions of the product, etc.) to discover the root cause of the problem and to use the collected data to inform decisions regarding how to attack the problem.

Educational leaders must go beyond one-dimensional analysis of test scores to drive their school improvement efforts. They must look at academic performance, as well as demographic, process, and perception data, to develop a better understanding of the interactions of the many factors that positively or negatively impact the functioning of a school organization. It is only through a thorough analysis of data gathered over time of the intersections of the four data types found in schools that educational leaders can accurately identify and address the factors that hinder improvement and positive change.

Chapter 3

Assessments and Their Role in Informing Instruction and the Learner

Frank S. Del Favero, PhD

For the past two decades, K–12 schools have had to deal with steadily increasing expectations and levels of accountability regarding student achievement. In many states, school districts as well as individual schools receive performance grades or ratings, which are based on a variety of measures with student performance on standardized test scores prominently weighted in the calculation of district and school performance ratings. Both principals and the instructional staff are acutely aware of the fact that, for the most part, student performance on standardized tests serves as a significant measure of school leaders' and teachers' effectiveness and, in some cases, based on an individual performance, could result in termination. With this in mind, it is obviously critical that educators focus on improving student academic performance on standardized tests.

STANDARDIZED TESTS AND LEARNING STANDARDS

Standardized tests, whether national, statewide, or locally generated, are all based on learning standards. For the sake of convenience, regardless of the never-ending metamorphosis of labels and names applied to these standards, this writer will use the term learning standards. Like standardized tests, learning standards can be either national or statewide, and are generally outcomes-based. Outcomes-based learning standards describe student competencies (i.e., what students are supposed to know [content] and be able to do [skills] by the end of each grade level).

Standardized tests are designed to measure student academic performance. It is important to note that their purpose is twofold: Firstly, appropriately analyzed standardized test scores (see chapter 1) inform the learner of the extent that she has acquired knowledge and skills relating to the goals and objectives addressed by the assessed learning standards. Secondly, standardized test scores can also inform instruction.

USING STANDARDIZED TESTS AND TEACHER-GENERATED CLASSROOM ASSESSMENTS TO INFORM THE LEARNER

The most common use of assessment scores, whether from standardized tests or from teacher-generated classroom assessments, is simply to provide students with an overall score. Standardized tests can be criterion referenced (i.e., usually based on a percentage of correct answers), norm referenced (i.e., percentile scores), or combinations of the two. Teacher-generated classroom assessments are generally criterion referenced.

Standardized Tests

Norm-referenced standardized test scores alone do little to inform the learner other than indicating where his performance score lies compared to other test takers or, in the case of criterion-referenced scores, the percentage of correct answers. These scores are best defined as outcome scores and provide very little if any information regarding the extent that the student has mastered and acquired the targeted content areas and skills defined by the specific assessed learning standards.

Rather than simply looking at a student's overall score on a standardized test, it is more informative to disaggregate a student's performance score on, for example, a standardized test in English Language Arts (ELA). In many cases, standardized test scores are broken down into performance on each of the targeted standards as well as their respective subelements. Our ELA example would provide scores on, for example, vocabulary, grammar, reading comprehension, comparing and contrasting literary characters, expository writing, listening comprehension, and so on. Individual scores in each of these tested areas provide the learner with a better and more detailed understanding of what they have learned. Individual scores on each of the learning standards and their subelements will help the learner to identify his strengths and weaknesses.

Identified strengths can help the learner know the extent that changes in study habits have impacted learning and can simply help the learner celebrate success. The identification of one's academic weaknesses can serve to help the student target areas for which intervention strategies to strengthen these areas are necessary.

Teacher-Generated Assessments

There is little difference between the ability of standardized test scores or teacher-generated classroom test scores to inform the learner of the extent that she has acquired and mastered the targeted knowledge and skills. Effective and meaningful feedback for the learner regarding performance on standardized and teacher-generated tests requires that academic performance data be disaggregated to provide separate scores on each of the learning standards targeted by these tests.

For teacher-generated assessments, the responsibility to disaggregate student performance scores by targeted learning standards lies with the classroom teacher. It is important to note, however, that this task is not necessarily as daunting and time-consuming as it may seem at first glance. Like the overall score of a standardized test, the grade, whether it be a letter grade or a percentage grade, is an output score or measure. When the learner receives a grade of B or a numerical grade of 85, these scores provide the learner little if any information that presents and describes the reasons why the student earned the awarded grade, nor does the student know what he should do to improve his performance on future assessments.

Teachers can provide their students valuable feedback by using analytic rubrics to grade essays and expository writing in all subject areas to evaluate their students' higher-order cognitive and writing skills. Properly constructed analytic rubrics serve as the foundation upon which teachers build a feedback system. Students can use this feedback system to further refine their study skills and thereby facilitate their acquisition of content-area knowledge and skills.

Analytic rubrics applied to any type of writing assessment can, for example, provide students constructive feedback regarding their writing mechanics (spelling, usage, punctuation, organization, etc.) and their level of understanding of the targeted content (the extent that the students used content knowledge to correctly complete the assessed task). Analytic rubrics inform the learner regarding the effectiveness of her study skills, and identify specific areas of strengths or weaknesses as they relate to writing skills and content.

Armed with this information a student with lower rubric scores in a content area can make appropriate adjustments as she prepares for future assessments.

USING STANDARDIZED TESTS AND TEACHER-GENERATED SUMMATIVE CLASSROOM ASSESSMENTS TO INFORM INSTRUCTION

Standardized tests and teacher-generated summative classroom assessments can and should also be used to inform instruction. It is important to note here that a detailed analysis of summative assessment and standardized test performance scores is almost exclusively used to inform instruction at the content area or program levels. Any meaningful analysis of standardized test scores should involve multiple measures of student performance on standardized tests over time. The analysis involves the disaggregation of test performance data by ethnicity, gender, educational classification (regular education, special education, 504 [other health impaired], or gifted and talented), language proficiency, socioeconomic status (SES), and teacher demographics.

The analysis should also provide information that details the percentages of students in a class with correct responses for each of the objective test questions and rubric scores for each of the extended response questions. Lastly but probably most importantly, the analysis should carefully consider the learning standard(s) and, if any, the associated subelement(s). The same process needs to be followed for teacher-generated summative assessments. Information gleaned from these analyses can help the teacher determine the effectiveness of classroom instruction, determine and/or refine appropriate instructional approaches and strategies, develop and refine lesson plans and formative assessments, evaluate, prioritize, and align the curriculum and related assessments with the learning standards, and lastly, identify and evaluate learning and instructional materials.

STANDARDIZED TESTS AND TEACHER-GENERATED SUMMATIVE CLASSROOM ASSESSMENTS

As mentioned in the introductory paragraph above, a great deal can be determined from an examination of standardized and teacher-generated summative classroom assessments. An analysis of standardized test scores or teacher-generated summative test scores must include at least three consecutive years of student performance data in order to identify an actionable trend. Looking at a "one-year snapshot" of student academic performance data does not provide enough information on which to create and institute an action plan. A one-year snapshot provides the observer with little more than information on academic performance for that given year. Unfortunately, at this stage, if the scores were found to be low, many schools would react and initiate interventions based on simple assumptions, guesses, and a perfunctory analysis of student performance data. This strategy most likely wastes dollars and effort while at the same time yielding more frustration and anxiety among the instructional staff than the desired academic improvement.

The goal of using summative classroom and standardized tests to inform instruction is to look for at least a three-year trend in the performance data. A negative trend can be said to exist if an analysis of three years of performance data reveals consistently low academic performance over time. A positive trend, on the other hand, is said to exist if scores remain consistently high over time. One should note that a positive trend would suggest that instructional strategies implemented in the past are successful and that it is time to celebrate success!

Once a negative trend has been identified, further analysis is necessary in order to gain a better understanding of exactly where the area(s) of concern lie(s). We would be concerned with low performance on an ELA assessment if we identified a three-year trend of low ELA performance scores. Rather than take some generalized unfocused steps to intervene, further, more detailed analysis is necessary. We need to dig further into the data to determine, for example, whether one student demographic group is performing at lower levels compared to other groups and determine the cause of the discrepancy. Teacher demographics, school process, and perception data all need to be looked at.

As a thought experiment, let us assume that student academic performance on the eighth-grade standardized test has consistently been falling over the last three years (a negative trend) as indicated by percent passing rates 59, 58, and 55. Disaggregating the data by ethnicity reveals some very interesting findings. The performance on the ELA test does indicate a negative trend for the overall school performance. However, the data disaggregated by ethnicity points to the existence of a significant academic performance gap. This gap indicates that white students are outperforming African-American and Hispanic students. Further analysis of the performance data needs to be undertaken in order to discover the reason(s) for the discrepancy in academic

Table 3.1.

| Ethnicity | Percent Passing Rates | | | |
	Year 1	Year 2	Year 3	Trend
White	80	82	85	positive
African-American	57	55	50	negative
Hispanic	40	38	30	negative
Total School:	**59**	**58**	**55**	**negative**

performance among the school's student ethnic groups. The focus of further analysis could possibly involve student, parental, and teacher perceptions regarding expectations, attendance rates among the various ethnicities, and a comparison of student discipline records disaggregated by ethnicity.

The structure and methodology of the analysis of performance, demographic, perception, and school process data can take a variety of forms, which are driven by the answers one seeks.

Having found a significant performance gap among white, African-American, and Hispanic students, the next step in the analysis is to determine if there are any intersections of the data. These intersections may involve, for example, intersecting school process data (instructional programs and/ or materials) and teacher demographic data (professional development) with performance scores on a variety of test questions that are disaggregated by teacher classes.

Interestingly, intersecting teacher professional development (school process data) with student academic performance disaggregated by teacher classes suggests that students of teachers who participated in professional development involving training in the area of analytical essay writing performed at higher academic levels compared to students whose teachers were not exposed to that training program. These findings inform instruction and are significant in that they present empirical evidence supporting and validating the professional development program that enables ELA teachers to further refine their instructional knowledge and skills in the area of analytical essay writing.

Table 3.2.

Eighth-Grade ELA Teacher	Percent passing rates on the extended response section of the ELA standardized test				
	Year 1	Year 2	Year 3	AET*	Trend
Teacher 1	80	82	85	yes	positive
Teacher 2	60	60	48	no	negative
Teacher 3	40	38	30	no	negative
Teacher 4	60	65	65	yes	positive
Total School:	**59**	**61**	**57**		**negative**

*Analytical Essay Training (AET)

THE UNDERSTANDING BY DESIGN FRAMEWORK
AND ITS ROLE IN ASSESSMENT

The tenets of the Understanding by Design (UbD) framework created by Grant Wiggins and Jay McTighe are, in this writer's opinion, the foundation on which effective teaching and learning rest. In the UbD framework, assessment of student outcomes plays a pivotal role in curriculum development and lesson planning. The driving force of the UbD framework is the backward design approach. Learning outcomes (i.e., what students are expected to know and be able to do), are the targets on which curriculum designers and lesson planers focus.

To illustrate the backward design approach, this writer has randomly selected from the Common Core State Standards (CCSS) in ELA for the eighth grade the speaking and listening ELA standard and one of the six strands contained therein. It reads as follows: "Analyze the purpose of information presented in diverse media and formats (e.g., visually, quantitatively, orally) and evaluate the motives (e.g., social, commercial, political) behind its presentation" (CCSS.ELA-LITERACY.SL.8.2).[1] The author offers below a sequential series of questions whose answers serve to guide the proper application of the backward design approach. The questions are as follows:

1. What is the learning outcome that is being targeted?

Answer: Analyze the purpose of information presented in diverse media and formats and evaluate the motives behind its presentation.

2. What content can I use to develop analytical and evaluation skills as stated in the standard?

Possible Answers: Syndicated book reviews from a local newspaper, YouTube videos of interviews with the author(s) of the selected work(s), book jacket(s) of the selected work(s), etc.

3. How will I determine the extent that my students have acquired and mastered the targeted analytical and evaluation skills?

Answer: Create an assessment that is aligned with the learning standard and that is to be administered at the end of the learning unit. It is important that this assessment accurately measures the targeted skills. In addition, it is important to measure student learning progress during the lessons. With this in mind, the teacher also creates formative assessments designed to inform instruction and the learner.

4. What do I need to teach my students in order for them to demonstrate acquisition and mastery of the targeted skills?

*Answer: At this point the teacher uses curricular goals and objectives
that are aligned with the standards to design and create the learning
activities that make up the daily lesson plans.*

The series of four questions that appear above serves as a guide to
understanding the UbD framework and the concept of designing assessments
and lessons with the end in mind. In summary, the teacher (1) examines the
learning standards and their respective outcomes, and (2) establishes the
learning and lesson objectives. Next, the teacher (3) designs and creates both
summative and formative assessments, and lastly, (4) uses the assessments
to form the lesson objectives to guide the development of the daily lesson
plans. It is easy to see that assessment/evaluation of student learning plays an
extremely important role in the teaching and learning process.

USING TEACHER-GENERATED FORMAL FORMATIVE
CLASSROOM ASSESSMENTS TO INFORM INSTRUCTION

Formative assessment is defined as any type of assessment that is administered
during the teaching and learning process. Remember, formative assessment
techniques are used while students are "forming" new knowledge and skills.
Formative assessment can be either informal, where no grades are recorded, or
it can be formal, where student grades are recorded and represent a student's
academic achievement. It the latter case, formal formative assessment is used
to measure the effectiveness of the teaching and learning processes.

Teacher generated assessments can be a valuable tool to evaluate student learning progress as students prepare throughout the academic year
to take the standardized and/or end-of-course tests prepared by national
testing organizations as well as those created or sponsored by state education departments. While in recent times it has become very common for
school districts to subscribe to computer software programs or locally created
assessments to measure student progress periodically throughout the academic year in the form of benchmark tests, teachers are often still required to
generate short quizzes and unit tests.

Thus far, this chapter has discussed the important role that the assessment/
evaluation of student academic progress plays. The Wiggins and McTighe
UbD framework and specifically the *backward design* element of that framework relies on assessment and evaluation to drive instruction. With this in
mind, it is critical that teacher-generated assessment instruments be carefully
designed and aligned with their respective learning standards.

The writer will again examine the CCSS eighth-grade ELA speaking and
listening standard, which was used as an example to demonstrate how the

backward design process is used to create courses and lessons that are aligned with the learning standards. This reexamination of the ELA learning standard will demonstrate how teachers can apply Bloom's Taxonomy of the Cognitive Domain to identify and classify the learning outcomes to generate classroom-appropriate assessments. It is critical that teachers be aware of the cognitive level of the targeted learning outcome.

BLOOM'S TAXONOMY OF THE COGNITIVE DOMAIN: A REFRESHER

As a refresher for the reader, the writer provides here a brief description of Bloom's Taxonomy of the Cognitive Domain. The cognitive domain is made up of six distinct levels of "knowledge" that describe the level of knowing. Each level builds on the previous one, increasing in complexity. At level 1, *remembering*, the learner is simply required to learn or memorize facts and information. At level 2, *understanding*, the learner is expected to be able to comprehend, describe in her own words, and compare information she has learned at the remembering level. Level 3, *applying*, builds upon the previous two levels, and the learner is expected to be able to apply what is remembered and understood to, for example, solve simple problems. A student performing at level 4, *analyzing*, is expected to use all that he has learned at the previous three levels to analyze a problem or scenario and break it down into its component parts. The learner functioning at level 5, *evaluating*, is expected to evaluate the component parts, picking and choosing which components, in her opinion, are usable and valid to support a position she may be expected to defend. At the final level (6, *creating*) the learner is expected to create something that addresses the assigned task, which could be a poem, a debate argument, an alternative method to solving a math or science problem, etc. At level 6 of the cognitive domain, the learner uses the findings or "knowledge" from each of the previous levels to create a product.

At or near the end of every academic year, students and their teachers have to deal with high-stakes testing, which includes End of Course (EOC) and state-level standardized tests that are aligned with the learning standards. This alignment addresses the learning outcomes on two fundamental levels: the content or topics addressed in the learning outcomes and the cognitive level(s) at which students are expected to perform. Our example learning standard reads as follows: "Analyze the purpose of information presented in diverse media and formats (e.g., visually, quantitatively, orally) and evaluate the motives (e.g., social, commercial, political) behind its presentation" (CCSS.ELA-LITERACY.SL.8.2).[2]

A careful reading of our example learning outcome above shows that eighth-grade students are expected to master specific knowledge and skills. They are accountable for (1) *analyzing* the purpose of information presented in diverse media formats. This particular outcome also requires the learner to *evaluate* the motives of the various forms of media. In Bloom's Taxonomy of the Cognitive Domain, analyzing is at the fourth of the six levels and evaluating is at the fifth and second-to-last level in the taxonomy. This implies that the teacher has to plan and deliver lessons and assessments which will prepare the learner and help him develop and refine analytical and evaluating skills as well as measure the learner's academic progress throughout the teaching and learning processes.

In order for the learner to acquire analytical and evaluating skills, the teacher must begin the process at the remembering, understanding, and applying (levels 1, 2, and 3) stages by presenting factual information that, in this example, is presented by a variety of media types and formats. At these stages of the teaching and learning process, the teacher presents the content so that the students can begin to develop a basic understanding of the content. At these beginning stages, the teacher employs instructional strategies whereby the students start to become familiar with the content.

The teacher next focuses on enabling the students to further develop their knowledge so that they are able to comprehend and understand the content by using their own words to describe and compare and contrast the various elements of the material. At the next level, applying, the teacher uses modeling and guided practice to make sure the students are able to solve simple problems based on the content.

During instruction at the first three levels of Bloom's Taxonomy, the teacher uses informal formative assessment strategies (no grades are recorded) to evaluate and measure the extent that students are acquiring knowledge and skills of the content during lesson presentations and learning activities. The teacher also uses formal formative assessments (grades are recorded) to measure the level of student mastery of the presented content. These formative assessments are usually in the form of teacher-generated, and in some cases, commercially generated unit/chapter tests and quizzes. The format of assessments during the *remembering*, *understanding*, and *applying* levels of the cognitive domain tend to be classified as objective questions. They are typically in the form of multiple-choice and short fill-in-the-blank questions.

It is extremely important the teacher realize that the level of instruction and assessments should be in direct alignment with the learning outcomes. In our example, the learning outcomes clearly state that the student is expected to analyze and evaluate. Learning activities therefore need to progress beyond the first three levels of the cognitive domain and address the targeted higher-order thinking skills. The teacher has to present lessons with learning activities that help students develop and refine their analytical and evaluating knowledge and skills. Students should participate in learning activities involving actual products from a variety of media formats so that they can analyze the content of the medium to determine its motive.

They should also use their analysis to evaluate the content and form an opinion. Assessments at the analyzing and evaluating cognitive domain levels are often classified as subjective and generally consist of extended or constructed response questions. Since there is no one specific answer that would apply to the question the rater uses a rubric and subjective judgment to assess the correctness and quality of student responses.

Unfortunately, because it is easier to teach and assess students at the lower levels of Bloom's Taxonomy, many teachers tend to concentrate their efforts and assessments on the first three levels of the cognitive domain and fail to progress on to the level(s) expressed in the learning outcome standards. Since the EOC and national- and state-level standardized assessments are very closely aligned with the learning outcomes, students whose teachers did not teach and evaluate them at the appropriate cognitive levels do not perform well on these assessments.

Not only do the students suffer as a result, but school performance ratings continue to stagnate year after year unless something is done to stop the downward slide. Teachers, curriculum supervisors, department heads, and principals all have to make a continuous, concerted effort to make certain that curricula, lesson plans, classroom instruction, and formative assessments are all closely aligned with the content knowledge and skills expressed in the learning standards with regard to the stated cognitive level(s).

USING INFORMAL CLASSROOM QUESTIONING TECHNIQUES TO INFORM INSTRUCTION

It is important to note that formative assessment can also be "informal" whereby the instructor informally assesses the rate of student learning during the lesson. The goal of informal formative assessment is to inform instruction. Grading and grades should not be involved in the informal formative assessment process.

One of the most common informal formative assessment techniques is known as "checking for understanding." A teacher accomplishes this by posing questions that serve to check the extent that students can explain, in their own words, the content and concepts of the lesson. In addition to posing questions to individual students, the teacher can ask the students to select a partner and to explain to their respective partner, in their own words, the content/concepts just presented. During these "pair and shares" the teacher circulates throughout the room listening to the discussions. The quality of student responses to the teacher's checking for understanding questions and/ or the "pair and shares" informs the teacher regarding the progression and effectiveness of the lesson. The teacher uses this information to make real-time decisions whether to

- continue with the lesson,
- stop, regroup, and reteach using a different instructional strategy, or
- identify in order to assist individual students experiencing difficulties understanding the material.

The teacher can also use the "pair and share" process to seek out students who engaged in one or two conversations she heard while monitoring conversations and ask these students to share with the entire class what they discussed during the "pair and share" activity. Having students state in their own words their understanding of the concepts presented by the teacher is an effective method of assessing the progress of the lesson, and informing instruction. It is also effective in that it informs the learners of where they are in the learning process.

USING INFORMAL CLASSROOM QUESTIONING TECHNIQUES TO INFORM THE LEARNER

Most, if not all, educators can understand and value the concept of using informal formative classroom assessment to inform instruction. They understand that it is important to constantly monitor the rate of learning and hence the effectiveness of the learning activity as well as the instructional strategies employed. They realize that is important to modify the lesson "on the fly" based on learner feedback. Unfortunately, it appears that much more attention is placed on test scores and their impact as measures of teacher effectiveness. There is not enough discussion about using formative (both formal and informal) and summative assessments/evaluations to guide and inform the learner.

Teacher feedback to students needs to go beyond a number or letter grade followed by a "smiley face," or a gold or silver or some other color star. If a student receives a letter grade of B or a number grade of 85 on her paper or lab report, she has a need and a right to know the reasons why she received such a grade. The teacher has to provide some type of feedback that informs the student what she has done well (her areas of strength) as well as areas that need attention so that on the next assessment, she knows exactly what needs improving and, as a result, knows which areas to place extra attention and effort on in order to show academic progress. An analytic rubric is the best method for providing students with feedback for any type of assessment requiring a constructed response.

For objective-type tests where there is only one acceptable response, at first glance meaningful feedback might seem impractical or impossible. Let's take, for example, a simple objective math quiz. Traditionally the teacher simply notes if the student's answer is either correct or incorrect, an appropriate number of points are deducted, and the student does not know why or the type of mistake made. A simple check mark informs neither the teacher nor the student of the type of mistake made or how to avoid it next time.

This can be remedied by a very simple technique that can be used in all subjects and is not limited to this math example. With every teacher-generated objective test or quiz the teacher can simply create two or three columns in the right or left margins of the assessment. At the top of each column the teacher enters a code representing the type of mistake the student has made. In this example of a math quiz, the teacher might label one column as "cka" (check answer), a second column as "mfa" (math facts), and the next as "for" (formula). Next, as she grades the quiz the teacher places a checkmark in the appropriate column for each incorrect answer.

When the student receives and reviews his graded quiz, he may note that many of his errors have checks in the "cka" column. This informs him that those errors were due to the fact that he did not carefully check his answers. He learns that the correct answer is 4.2 and not 42 and that his mistake was leaving out the decimal point. He now knows that his errors mainly lie in the fact that he did not carefully review his work or accurately enter his answers on the answer sheet.

After having graded all of the quizzes, the teacher can easily tally the types of errors made by the students and review or reteach appropriately. Feedback to the students during the teacher's use of informal formative questioning techniques can also be instrumental in informing the learner.

During instruction, a student can make note of the content of the teacher's checking for understanding questions and pairing and sharing topics. The questions posed and the topics discussed are all indicators of learning and assessment targets. A concerted effort must be made to make students aware of the extent that rubrics, grading techniques, the teacher's informal questions, and discussion topics inform them of the teacher's expectations regarding their knowledge of and skills in regard to the course content.

CHAPTER SUMMARY

This chapter has discussed the importance of aligning curriculum, lesson plans, instructional strategies, and classroom assessment with the learner outcomes of national/state learning standards. It has also presented a brief review of Bloom's Taxonomy and the various levels of knowledge in the cognitive domain, as well as the role that they play in the alignment of instruction and assessment. With all of this in mind, an effective leader will

1. help her teachers to plan lessons and assessments that are closely aligned with the learning standards as they relate to the grade level competencies of their respective grade levels and subject area content;
2. constantly monitor lesson plans and classroom instruction to make certain that instruction and assessment not only matches the content but also the cognitive level stated in the learner outcomes in the state/national standards;
3. make certain that the instructional staff is fully aware of and implements strategies to use formal and informal formative and summative assessments to inform instruction; and
4. ensure that teachers provide detailed feedback that informs the learner in a manner that identifies the learner's areas of success as well as areas needing extra effort and attention.

NOTES

1. http://www.corestandards.org/ELA-Literacy/SL/8/2/.
2. http://www.corestandards.org/ELA-Literacy/SL/8/2/.

Chapter 4

Evaluating Instruction

Amanda Shuford Mayeaux, EdD

LESSON VIGNETTE

One April morning Mr. Bradford, the principal, and Mrs. Smith, the assistant principal, entered Mr. John's sixth-grade English Language Arts class for a formal observation of his teaching. Mr. Bradford sat in the back corner with his pad of paper and pencil, while Mrs. Smith sat in the opposite back corner with her computer. Each had a unique style of scripting the lesson. Mr. John, a consistently strong teacher, began the lesson with a funny video clip. After the two-minute clip ended, he said to the children, "For the next minute, do a quick-write and jot down every connection you can make to yesterday's lesson." When the timer went off, Mr. John said, "Now, one minute to write your predictions about how this relates to today's topic." The time rang out again and Mr. John directed, "Partner talk! Partner A, explain how this clip relates to yesterday's discussion. Partner B, predict how you think this clip will relate to today's discussion. Two minutes—go!"

The children began chatting very animatedly. Mr. John reset the visual timer going on the screen and then began to walk around the room. He stopped at several desks and squatted down to listen. Mrs. Smith noticed he jotted notes on a clipboard after standing up each time. At the end of the two minutes, the time sounded, and all children stopped talking immediately and turned to the front. Mr. John said, "Weekly leaders, stand up and testify!" Five students stood, and a lively discussion followed with the weekly leaders responding and calling on others to share.

Mr. John explained the objectives of the day, "Your discussion was spot-on. You made some very powerful connections. Today, we will work together to draw inferences about character actions. Listening to your discussions, I heard words like foreshadowed, which made me smile."

Mr. John began the body of the lesson by stating, "I know some of you have read ahead, because you just have to know what is happening to our main character. Today we will use a short story of the same genre to understand how character actions help us infer ideas in the text. First, I will model how I think about text and make inferences using this paragraph. Everyone should be facing me with your pens ready to write. Then you will do the same with your partner and finally alone."

The rest of the lesson followed a similar style as Mr. John offered short bits of direct instruction by modeling his thinking as he analyzed a paragraph of text. Some questions were intertwined before students moved effortlessly into pairs and analyzed two paragraphs using the given thinking questions Mr. John had modeled. As the students worked, Mr. John moved around the room, again squatting down and listening as he made notes on his clipboard. Then Mr. John gave the students a longer selection to analyze independently. After they analyzed the selection, the students moved through a chalk talk where each poster had a significant quotation from the extended text. Students were to make connections and predictions from the quotations.

At the end of the class, Mr. John asked students to complete a three-two-one exit slip with three questions they had for the main character, two things they would do differently if they were the main character, and one prediction they could make about how this passage would impact the main character's outcome. The lead students moved to grab index cards and pass them out. The students filled out the cards and placed them in a basket as they exited the class. Many students thanked Mr. John and said things like, "Have a great day!"

Mr. Bradford and Mrs. Smith returned to their respective offices and scored the lesson. The following morning, they met to find consensus concerning the scores. The two evaluators had aligned scores up until the subcategory of grouping. Mr. Bradford scored Mr. John a one out of four and Mrs. Smith scored Mr. John a four out of four.

Mr. Bradford was aghast. "How can you give him a four, you never give anyone a four!"

Mrs. Smith replied, "First, I did not give him anything, I think he earned it. Why did you score him a one?"

Mr. Bradford said, "Well, the rubric clearly states teachers model group expectations. I did not see him model any expectations. He just told them to move."

Mrs. Smith maintained her calm tone and explained, "It is April! When he told the students to move into group activities, what happened every time?"

Mr. Bradford thought for a moment and replied, "They did it immediately . . . all of them."

Mrs. Smith smiled and said, "Exactly."

EVALUATING INSTRUCTION

Evaluating instruction is more than a simple rubric checklist of teacher behaviors. Each teacher has an individual style and each class has a specific culture and climate. Expecting every lesson to look a specific way is to attempt to standardize the art of teaching, which is a very human process and therefore cannot be standardized. Though there are defining elements of highly effective teaching, the evidence is not found only in the actions and words of the teacher. The true evidence is found in the actions and words of the students.

In the given scenario, Mr. Bradford was looking for the rote connection to the rubric. He expected Mr. John to model the partner talk, including who was to be Partner A and who was to be Partner B, what they were to do, and the use of the time. Mrs. Smith recognized partner talk was a seamless part of the class culture, because Mr. John did not have to do anything but tell the students to move into the protocol. Mrs. Smith also recognized that what happens in a classroom in April is often much different than what happens in a classroom in September. Mr. John had clearly modeled these protocols early in the year and used these continuously throughout the year.

Mrs. Smith's understanding of the evidence of effective teaching and learning being found in the actions and words of students was diametrically opposed Mr. Bradford's understanding of an evaluation being solely about the teacher's words and actions. When the two evaluators compared their scripting notes, Mr. Bradford had written down each word Mr. John had said. Conversely, Mrs. Smith had typed notes that included the teacher's words and actions, students' words and actions, and notes about things found around the classroom. She had even taken pictures of the chalk talk discussion pages. Mrs. Smith had also asked to see the exit tickets and had taken a few pictures of some.

STUDENT-CENTERED EVALUATIONS

When an evaluator has a deep understanding of teaching and learning, the evaluation becomes a discussion tool between teacher and evaluator. Evaluations are not "gotcha" opportunities meant to punish teachers.

The goals of evaluations are to

- actively develop expert teaching and learning in each classroom,
- offer consistent opportunities for collaborative dialogue in the school, and
- develop a school culture in which reflective teaching is honored and encouraged.

These goals are achieved when evaluations are student-centered and aligned to the goals of each classroom and of the school. Student-centered evaluations look at the evidence through the lens of the students rather than simply the behaviors of the teachers. This perspective eliminates the so-called dog and pony show teachers may assume evaluations to be and allows for discussion based upon evidence. Student-centered evaluations of teaching focus on five distinct areas of the classroom.

1. Lesson alignment to content standards and student needs
2. Implementation and impact of chosen instructional strategies
3. Application of formative assessment and feedback throughout the lesson
4. Students' active engagement in the lesson
5. A classroom culture conducive to teaching and learning

Regardless of the evaluation rubric being used by an administrator, applying a student-centered lens to these five areas allows an evaluator to see the big picture of what is happening in the instruction. In the vignette with Mr. Bradford and Mrs. Smith, Mr. Bradford was compartmentalizing each element, while Mrs. Smith saw the lesson not only as a whole, but also as a small piece of the entire year. Mrs. Smith used the evidence of students moving seamlessly into group work to infer that Mr. John had not only taught the structures, but also consistently and effectively used these structures as part of his teaching. The structures led to rich discussions, which were now part of the classroom culture.

Student-centered evidence will be found in three places: student questions and discussions, student actions, and student work. These three are foundational to the five areas as evaluators seek evidence of teaching and learning.

LESSON ALIGNMENT

Lesson planning is more than the simple completion of the lesson plan template. An expert teacher is a better decision-maker, because he/she understands which decisions are important and which are not (Hattie, 2003). Borko and Livingston (1990) found in their study of expert and novice teachers that expert teachers had no written lesson plans, but all could easily describe mental plans for their lessons. These mental plans typically included a general sequence of lesson components and content. This is not to suggest the elimination of written plans, but to understand that expert teachers have a deeper understanding of their lesson than a written plan may offer.

Expert teachers have developed curricula based on standards that align to national expectations (Good & Brophy, 2008). However, effective planning and teaching is more than simple alignment. An expert teacher can identify essential representations of their subject(s) and have deeper representations about the teaching and learning of their subjects (Hattie, 2003). Expert teachers understand how to make connections between ideas and other disciplines. They also understand how to use instructional time carefully by differentiating between critical content and less important content. Expert teachers plan their time to focus student learning on what is important (Good & Brophy, 2008). Marzano (2008) states that when effective teachers introduce new content they link the content to prior learning, preview the new learning, add narratives and anecdotes, and also teach the content in small chunks in order to allow students to digest. The opportunity to learn is a tremendous current variable in the United States, which up to this point has not had a common curriculum (NGA, 2011).

In the face of uniformity and scripted programs, the teacher is slowly being eliminated from the decision-making process of what is taught in each classroom. Standardization is often seen as a way to foolproof education, but each class is unique and each child is unique. Rather than standardize lessons, teachers should be equipped to develop expertise through evaluations and collaborative dialogue.

Student-centered evaluations seek evidence that teachers have aligned the lessons to not only the standards, but also student needs. The sources of evidence include student questions and discussions, student actions, and student work.

Student questions and discussions can assist an evaluator in understanding if the content is both challenging and attainable. When learning new content, evidence of students struggling does not necessarily mean the teacher has not scaffolded the lesson correctly. The struggle may lead to strong conclusions, new connections, deeper understanding, or even more questions. The lack of struggle may indicate the lesson is below the level of the students. Students wrestling with content means that learning is occurring. The expert teacher will facilitate this struggle toward success by scaffolding the lesson toward the goal.

Student actions are another strong indicator of alignment. When the lesson is aligned to the standards and to student needs, actions align. For example, during Mr. John's class, he asked students to make predictions and connections, which they did successfully. The actions observed included the students quickly turning to the partners, engaging in discussion, and producing relevant predictions and connections. This demonstrated that students retained the previous learning and were able to make some inferences towards future learning.

Student work is the gold standard for alignment. In the given lesson, evidence from student work could be found in the connections and predication slips, the posted chalk talk discussion, and the exit tickets. For each of these an evaluator could match the questions to curriculum standards and the student work to levels of standards. The evaluator could also evaluate if the work met students' needs by the level of engagement and progress towards the lesson goal.

INSTRUCTIONAL STRATEGIES

Any teacher with more than a year of experience can confirm each class is unique and has unique needs. The choice of instructional strategies demonstrates a teacher's understanding of both the standards and the needs of students. Mrs. Smith returned to Mr. John's class during fifth period and noticed there was no poster paper up for a chalk talk. Curious, she decided to stay for a few minutes to see what happened. At the point in the lesson where the chalk talk had occurred in the morning, Mr. John instead directed the students to move to groups of four and complete a Think–Write Round Robin (Kagen). Mrs. Smith inquired after class about this choice. Mr. John replied, "Oh, fifth period is very heavy in energy, particularly after lunch. I have found the chalk talk usually devolves into chaos, but the use of a Think–Write Round Robin keeps everyone focused and on target, while allowing the students to have a nonverbal discussion about the topic."

Often teachers choose the in vogue instructional strategy without processing the why and how of the strategy. Mr. John clearly understood the needs of his students and made a change in instructional strategy without compromising the level of the discussion. Instructional strategy choices are also where a teacher's understanding of individual student needs is evident.

Differentiation has been an educational buzzword for many years with numerous sterilized suggested methods, but a teacher's use of differentiation is solely based upon the needs of individual children at a given moment in a given class. In Mr. John's class he met individual student needs by the way he paired the students. He considered students' academic needs, but also their personalities and social-emotional needs. For example, Martha is a recovering stroke victim, who is very shy. Mr. John paired her with Angelina, who is very compassionate and articulate. Mr. John also modified the exit ticket for two students by allowing them to choose which questions to answer from the three-two-one activity. David, however, chose to answer the questions from all three areas even when he was not required to do so. Mr. John also gave his struggling readers a modified text and his higher-level readers a longer text.

Instructional strategies should encourage student questions and discussion. The two elements may be verbal or written. For example, in the opening of the lesson, Mr. John had students write first, then share with partners, and then share as a whole. Throughout the lesson, Mr. John changed instructional strategies approximately every ten minutes. Students moved from individual to partner to whole-group learning and then from whole to partner to individual learning throughout the lesson.

The purposes of instructional strategies are to engage students and to create evidence for teachers to assess student learning to create opportunities for teacher and peer feedback. In this lesson, Mr. John created numerous opportunities to observe student actions, as well as their discussions and questions.

Instructional strategies create a record of student thinking for peer and teacher feedback. After this class, Mr. John would have his anecdotal notes he made throughout the class, the students' small group and individual group work, the chalk talk posters, and the exit tickets. Each of these offer him clues as to the strengths and weaknesses the students have with the content. He may then adapt the following day's lesson to overcome issues and deepen already existing understandings. The student work can also be an opportunity for rich discussions in the postevaluation interviews.

ASSESSMENT AND FEEDBACK

Instructional strategies lead to student work, which teachers may use to assess learning and offer feedback. Effective teachers provide plenty of time for students to practice and apply their new learning. Hattie (2003) states giving critical feedback is the most important action a teacher offers in a classroom and can provide a 1.13 gain in student achievement. During the practice phase students are offered opportunities to try skills in a variety of contexts and formats, which moves the learning to a high level of understanding (Good & Brophy, 2008).

Marzano (2008) clearly defines actions effective teachers use during the practice and application process, including a review of the content, allowing students to review and revise notes, and effectively using the homework. Student achievement is increased when teachers allow students to examine content for similarities and differences and examine their own logic. Through these types of activities, the effective teacher is helping students deepen their understanding through feedback to a conceptual level with a focus on fluent knowledge.

Assessment should be occurring throughout every lesson, not simply as an end of the week quiz or unit exam. Mr. John created multiple opportunities to assess his students and to give feedback. Throughout the lesson, students were able to pose questions and to engage in rich discussions, both in small groups and as a whole class. Mr. John also had many opportunities to listen to these conversations, ask clarifying or thought-provoking questions, and give feedback.

Feedback may occur in multiple layers. Students may implement self-feedback where they analyze their own work, compare/contrast their work to a standard, or refine what they have already completed. Peer feedback impacts student learning on two levels. First, peer feedback offers the recipient thoughts about the work, but peer feedback also requires the student evaluator to analyze and apply her own understanding in order to give the feedback. This deepens the student evaluator's knowledge and skills.

Finally, teacher feedback is important to the learning process in the classroom. Feedback may be verbal and/or written. Feedback may occur individually or to a group. The important part is that feedback occurs and pushes the students' progress toward mastery. Feedback is also where a teacher's understanding of differentiating instruction is evident. An expert teacher will give specific, clear, and purposeful feedback to each individual.

Student actions also offer evidence for evaluators of the effective use of assessment and feedback. When teachers circulate and give feedback during instruction, student actions should demonstrate the result of the feedback. The feedback may be about many lesson elements including the work, management, group interaction, and engagement. For example, during the group discussion, Mr. John noticed Melissa was not sharing during the discussion. He went over to the group and listened, before asking Melissa what she thought. The rest of the group quieted, and Melissa shared. Mr. John praised her and then reminded the group of the discussion protocol procedures. Melissa engaged more productively as the other group members used the protocol effectively.

Student work is a treasure trove for the impact and implementation of feedback. While observing a class, the evaluator notices a teacher giving specific verbal feedback to a student. If this feedback is received, the student work should show the evidence. For example, Mr. John noticed one group was not citing evidence to support their thinking. He went over to the group and chatted with them for a few minutes. Mrs. Smith examined the student work after class to see if the verbal feedback transferred to their work. She found that not only did the group cite evidence, the individuals in the group also cited evidence in their individual work. Feedback should have an impact and the impact should be evident.

STUDENT ENGAGEMENT

During the discussion between Mr. Bradford and Mrs. Smith, Mr. Bradford shared that he felt like student engagement was very low during the part of the lesson where students were reading individually. Mrs. Smith was surprised and asked him to explain his thinking.

"First, no one was active. They were just sitting there looking at the paper. I did see some make notes, but the rest looked like they were daydreaming to me. To top it all off, all Mr. John did was walk around making notes about who knows what."

"You believe reading is not engagement?"

"Well, reading isn't very active, and kids really could fake it," replied Mr. Bradford.

Mrs. Smith asked, "What would be the evidence they are not faking it?"

"I guess they could talk about what they read and answer questions, but there were no worksheets. I guess you don't agree with me. What did you see?"

Mrs. Smith thought for a moment and said, "I am not sure if you noticed, but during the lesson I walked around the room a few times. One of those times was during individual reading. I noticed things like students tracking the text with their eyes. A few made notes in the margins, while others highlighted parts of the text. When the students moved to the chalk talk, I read responses where students cited examples from the text, which gave me further evidence they had read the material. After you left, I stayed and read through the exit tickets to gain an understanding of where students were in their progress toward the goal. According to the evidence I found, student engagement was extremely high throughout the lesson. Finally, I asked Mr. John to see his notes and he shared a very comprehensive list of notes he had on each student. He is bringing those to the postconference tomorrow."

Student engagement is often an element of classroom evaluation left to the opinion of the evaluator. Some evaluators desire to see students moving and shouting out answers in a rote manner. Some evaluators wish to see students seated and quietly working on assignments. Engagement is a multifaceted element within a classroom. The highest level of engagement is the engagement of the mind, which is often not as visible as actions. The evaluator must look deeply and thoroughly for student-centered evidence of strong mental engagement, but the evidence can be found.

The words of students found in their questions and discussions are one layer of evidence evaluators may use to understand the level of student engagement. Mrs. Smith recorded both the teacher's words and students' words in her script. She also sought the students' written words in the various records she took. Mrs. Smith used these words to gather evidence about not only if, but how, students engaged in the lesson, as well as how deeply they did so.

Student actions would seem to be easy to observe, but students actively reading appeared to Mr. Bradford to be disengaged. When students are reading or thinking, often there is no visible action occurring; therefore, evaluators must seek other sources to find evidence of student engagement. Conversely, sometimes students' actions are lively and highly engaging, but lead to little progress toward the goal.

One example of this would be when students are engaged in a superficial assignment or "fluff" work. "Fluff" work is pretty highly engaging but does little to push students toward a deeper understanding of the content. Mr. John's next-door neighbor, Mrs. Janet, was teaching what she believed to be the same lesson, as the pair often coplanned together. Instead of having students read silently, the students read aloud as a whole class, pausing every few minutes to complete a fill-in-the-blank reading guide. Mr. Bradford would have seen students engaged, but if he considered the standard, this "highly engaging" activity did not meet the standard of students reading and making inferences independently.

Student work is the final piece of the engagement puzzle. When examining student work, we often look for completeness, adherence to the directions, and the answer, always the answer. However, student work gives us much more information when the work is created with thought and alignment to the goals. In Mr. John's classroom, students' exit tickets were the only student work the evaluators could use to assess student learning.

One of the issues with student work is fluff. Beware of the fluff and assignments designed to simply keep students busy. Student work should be rigorous and match the standards, but more importantly, student work should inform the teacher and the students about student thinking and deepening of understanding. Student work and listening to student talk is the evidence teachers should use to make decisions about next steps.

In the postinterview, evaluators have the opportunity to understand the connections teachers are making between what happened in the classroom, the student work, and the learning goals of the lesson. These connections are key to the next steps teachers plan.

In the postinterview Mrs. Smith asked Mr. John, "How do you think the lesson went?"

Mr. John replied, "Overall, the lesson went well. I am pleased with discussions I heard in several of the groups, particularly group two. This group has Adalie in it and she often struggles to keep up in discussions, but I gave her a little bit of extra background knowledge through a video the previous day. This really helped her. I made some notes while walking around and I heard Adalie ask questions and make a few comments. These were all connected to the discussion and she even took notes. Also, the group's leader,

Susan, is a great coach and facilitator. Adalie did not take the modification for the exit ticket and did all three questions. She did not make a prediction about the main character, but rather her favorite character. The prediction was a little basic, but this is tremendous progress for Adalie."

Mrs. Smith said, "Wow! I am excited for Adalie and for you. Where will you go from here with Adalie?"

Mr. John thought for a moment, "Adalie is not the only one struggling to make connected predictions. I knew the kids were struggling with these from the previous lesson, but when I examined the charts from the chalk talk and the exit tickets, I see loosely based predictions with little detail. About half of the students are offering weak connections, a quarter are on target, and the final quarter have strong work. The natural thing to do would be to group these together and have a chat, but I think I have a better idea. Tomorrow I am pasting the strong exit ticket responses on chart paper. Then each author will stand by his or her poster while the rest of the class rotates in small groups from one poster to the next. The author will do a "think-aloud" for the groups. The groups will listen and record what they are hearing. Then the students will get into groups of three and find connections between the "think-alouds" they have heard. I will have the authors rotate and give feedback."

The postconference continued with similar types of questions and discussion. At the end, Mrs. Smith shared a strength and weakness, as required by the district.

There were many strengths in this lesson, but of course, I have to choose one, so I will choose your overall lesson planning. Everything flowed well together and the students were never unengaged. I could have chosen engagement, but the reason they were engaged was how you structured things. As for a weakness, I really had a hard time choosing one, but through our discussion, I think you have the same idea. You have mentioned using different texts and allowing the students to choose the short text for their independent practice. This would allow student choice. Students would be exposed to some additional readings, which may push them to read another book. Different texts also may allow you to group students by interest or even differentiate based on need. However, please do not fall into the trap where students are reading texts solely based on Lexile. Interest is a tremendous motivator.

As Mr. John left, Mr. Bradford, who had been sitting quietly throughout the postconference, smiled.

"You really make this look easy, but there are so many things going on. When I was trained to observe and evaluate, I was told to look for a hook, look for some direct instruction, some group work, and something to show kids did

know what they were doing. I kind of see it as a checklist in my head, but you, you see all the connections between the teacher and students. You see everything as clues to what is happening. I don't know how to do that."

"First of all, teaching is not a checklist. Teaching is a very intricate process every day, or at least it should be. I look at the facial expressions and body language of the students. I always watch the students. When we watch the teacher and only look to check off things on a list, we miss the magic of what should be happening. Anyone can stand before a class and give a performance that meets the elements on a list, but the best teachers are not performing. They are engrossed in the work and their students are the evidence," replied Mrs. Smith.

CLASSROOM CULTURE

Classroom culture is often confused with classroom management, but classroom culture is the sum of many elements. Classroom management impacts culture either positively or negatively. When a teacher has the lessons well planned, materials ready to go, and can facilitate the lessons so students are 100 percent engaged, the culture is impacted positively. However, many other elements impact the culture of a classroom. The teacher's attitude, words, and actions have tremendous impact on the culture. In the lesson observed, the words and actions of the teacher were clues to the culture of the classroom.

Students were an engaged part of the lesson from the beginning until the end. Not only were students engaged, but all voices were included. Mr. John used partner activities, chalk talks, and classroom discussions to allow everyone to share. Mr. John also set each student up for success by thinking through the lesson to make clear connections for the students. Student engagement demonstrated student willingness to participate, take risks, and wrestle with new content. Students were not passive receivers of information, but rather, part of the propulsion of the lesson. They were generating elements of the discussion.

Observers in such a classroom can note the actions of students by watching when students engage in partner talk, share individually, work in groups, complete independent tasks, and complete all types of other actions. What is critical is to watch and understand what students are doing rather than simply watching the teacher's actions.

In the observed lesson, students seamlessly moved into the various group structures, which indicated these structures and engagement were parts of the culture. Students came to Mr. John's class knowing they would be expected to engage through discussions and written work. The expectations were established and clear. When students are all engaged in the lesson, chances are the culture of the classroom is positive.

Student work also demonstrates evidence of positive classroom culture. Student work may be shown on the walls, but more importantly, observers should note how much effort students are putting into the work. Are they engaged? Are they giving detailed responses? Are they working together? Are they questioning and seeking to understand deeply? These observations are critical to understanding the culture.

CHAPTER SUMMARY

The majority of observation tools being used to evaluate teachers focus on teacher actions rather than student actions. When evaluators step back and examine students and their work, the elements of lessons, from alignment to engagement, become much clearer. The understanding of what is effective teaching and what is not may actually shift when we look at what students are saying and doing. Long gone are the days where teachers talk for an entire period and students take notes. Today's classrooms must be filled with highly engaged students, who are being challenged to think, problem-solve, and create new understandings. The only way to evaluate if these things are happening is to center evaluations around the students, rather than only the teacher.

Chapter 5

Evaluating Curriculum

Nancy P. Autin, PhD, and Tarrah C. Davis, EdD

The process of evaluating curriculum provides ongoing reflection in a learning environment focused on preparing students with enduring knowledge and skills to become well-rounded and successful individuals in everyday life. A discussion of this process is reflected throughout this chapter. It is critical to establish that several overlapping assumptions guide this chapter, each equally important.

One assumption is that school leaders will cultivate a school culture that promotes and values teamwork. The values and skills infused throughout the curriculum must first be fostered and supported in the community of adult learners: open-mindedness, flexibility, critical thinking, creativity, and problem-solving. Embedded in this assumption is the idea that all decisions are driven by shared beliefs as reflected in a school's vision for student learning.

A second assumption supports the belief that curriculum evaluation is ongoing. Assigning value to a school's instructional program is based on the intersecting needs of society, community, and students; needs change, and so must curriculum if it is to be relevant. While definite criteria are considered in evaluating a school's existing curriculum, relevance necessitates crossing boundaries to ensure fidelity to school goals and learner expectations throughout all grade levels and subject areas for all students.

It is gravely important that school leaders engage teachers and stakeholders in creating meaningful goals as reflected in the school's vision for school improvement. This third assumption provides everyone with a common understanding of what this ongoing process entails. It helps teachers see that curriculum evaluation is far more than simply reviewing a course or adding new activities and changing assessments.

The faculty learning forward activity included below will help put these assumptions and key elements of the evaluation process into perspective. The activity is intended to create reflective practitioners who have accepted the responsibility to prepare today's students for their evolving future. It is advised that the activity take place in conjunction with or after a review of philosophies (see next section).

FACULTY LEARNING AND LEADING ACTIVITY

You are appointed to a curriculum commission consisting of educators, civic and business leaders, and parents charged with the responsibility of designing a new curriculum for precollege schools in the United States, to be implemented by 2025. Your task as an expert educator is to provide substantive feedback on the following items at the curriculum commission's first meeting.

a. What educational philosophy would you adopt?
b. What vision will you propose for teaching and learning as we approach 2025?
c. What major goals will drive curriculum planning?
d. What learner needs and skills will be the focus of instruction? Will they remain the same as those already identified as twenty-first-century learner skills? Or will they be different?
e. Describe the learning environment. What will it look like?
f. How will the curriculum be organized? What will the core subjects be? Will there be distinct subjects or disciplines? What new subject areas, if any, would you propose?
g. How will the school year and day be organized?
h. Would schools still span K–12 grades or would you propose something different?

A well-planned strategy for implementing this activity will maximize the benefits for all involved. Decide in advance if all parts, (a)–(h), will be considered in a single professional learning gathering. Based on that decision, designate an approximate amount of time for considering all parts, (a)–(h), or a smaller amount of time if the plan includes revisiting the activity at subsequent faculty learning sessions. One strategy is to focus on individual reflection followed by team collaboration. The strategy outlined below uses individual reflection for item (a) and team collaboration for items (b)–(h).

1. Ask teachers to write their response to question (a). This is done independently.
2. Form teams of three or four in which members share a common philosophy.
3. Ask teams to compose a clear, concise, and single group response to items (b)–(h).
4. Tell teams to electronically submit one set of responses for items (b)–(h). This can be done using Google forms or some other application that gathers this data readily.
5. Display each team's response to question (b) to the entire group.
6. Use a strategy to analyze common themes related to item (b), the proposed vision for 2025.

Questions can also be grouped and considered in later professional learning sessions. For example, items (c), (d), and (e) may generate robust discussion among teachers of the same discipline. Item (e) may be approached in grade bands, such as pre-K–2, lower elementary, upper elementary or middle, and high school. The overarching goal is to prompt creative thinking and to honor the input of teachers, the individuals who have the greatest impact on student learning and achievement.

PHILOSOPHY AND GOALS

What philosophy is driving the curriculum? A meaningful review of curriculum begins by pondering the educational backdrop or philosophy that best characterizes learning and the learning environment within a school. What knowledge should be mastered? What skills are essential? What values will drive the curriculum? What is the role of the teacher? How is the student viewed in the learning process? Whose needs drive curricular decisions? Unless school leaders respond clearly to these questions, engaging others in evaluating the curriculum will likely be a shallow process.

When asked what philosophy, or combination of philosophies, best describes a school and its programs, school leaders and teachers often display uncertainty. Where do educators go to find answers? To resolve this dilemma, Henson (2015) proposes that "knowing one's personal philosophies empowers educators."[1] This personal introspection will better equip school leaders and teachers to engage in robust discussions, leading to philosophical systems that fit the purpose of school and how it functions today.

Leading the faculty in an activity to review major underpinnings of schools in the United States will be beneficial. Something as simple as a Four Corners Activity will work. Use keywords or phrases from the descriptions below to motivate thinking and prompt discussion.

- *Essentialism* focuses on teaching the basic elements of academic and moral knowledge. Essentialists emphasize a conservative intellectual and moral standards approach to what is taught and how students are taught. Service learning and school-to-work programs are okay but must fit within core subjects. The goal is to stabilize society by teaching literacy, numeracy, and social norms to all students throughout all grades.
- *Perennialism* focuses on knowledge that has withstood the test of time. The curriculum emphasizes classical literature, history, philosophy, science, and fine arts. The curriculum emphasizes reading, writing, and arithmetic. Perennialists argue that their goal is to teach students to think, and the way to do this is to combine classical subjects with the basics.
- The goal of *Progressivism* is the development of the whole child. Students' personal experiences, interests, and learning styles are important in the instructional process. This philosophy purports that students create their own understanding; teachers are facilitators or coaches.
- *Reconstructionism* believes that education should focus on correcting social issues in society by teaching students how to analyze social problems and take meaningful action to resolve these issues. Reconstructionism promotes student inquiry and dialogue within the context of problem-solving and creative thinking.[2]

The good energy comes naturally when philosophy, learner needs, and instruction and assessment are working in concert. All are critical to achieving the vision established for ongoing improvement. The philosophy influencing the instructional program must reflect shared principles consistent with the vision of the school. Instruction and assessment must take advantage of teachers' strengths and student differences.

DESIGNING GOALS FOR STUDENT LEARNING

The topics included in a unit on setting goals for student learning are all equally important: Know what matters, know the difference, ask the right questions, and communicate priorities and progress.

KNOW WHAT MATTERS

Nearly seven decades ago, Ralph Tyler wrote, "Education is a process of changing the behavior patterns of people" (1971).[3] Today, changing behavior patterns remains a focus. With the explosion of knowledge and new technologies, different behavior patterns are needed to function successfully as compared to years past. Setting goals to impact change is invigorating; it is akin to preparing for an exciting Broadway stage performance. Rehearsals include planning, interventions, making adjustments, and setting new goals. After some time, the curtain rises. Learning forward is the theme. A host of main characters are collaborating: Facilitator, Assessment Guru, Creators, and Innovators.

Vision and philosophy are the umbrella under which goals are formulated and protected. Throughout the learning process, those protected, students, must know what is expected: making connections to real-life situations, thinking critically about next steps, asking questions, and using resources to generate ideas and create new products. In this environment, the goals, including the deep thinking and the doing, serve as the foundation for establishing meaningful and lasting learning.

Determining goals—that is, setting new goals for student learning and school effectiveness—begins with the careful and honest review of school data. It involves the entire cast working together: school leaders and researchers (directors), instructional facilitators and assessment gurus, creators, and inventors (faculty, staff, students), and the audience (parents and community). Individual and community needs matter. Far-reaching societal needs influence goals as students share citizenship beyond geographic boundaries.

KNOW THE DIFFERENCE

Overarching goals are different from instructional objectives; they are broad and typically not subject-area specific. Goals take into account the overall needs of the student population. The needs of subpopulations, as identified in data analysis, may likewise be the focus of a school's goals.

In the learning environment, it is easy for practitioners to devote most of their time to planning instructional activities. While this is an important phase of lesson planning, curriculum evaluation takes into account how learner activities contribute to achieving learning goals. Activities will make sense to students in the context of what one is to know and be able to do during and at the end of the learning. McTighe and Wiggins (2013) state the critical question as, "To what extent do our teaching practices align with our goals?"[4]

ASK THE RIGHT QUESTIONS

By asking the right questions up front, navigating the process with the end in mind will culminate in a meaningful draft of goals. Although not exhaustive, these questions will generate beginning discussion in the goal-setting process.

- Based on the data, what must be the immediate goals for improved learning?
- What teaching and learning theories do we now know that cause us to see and do things differently?
- What structures must be in place to ensure that all students attain the knowledge and skills needed for success in a future world that is unknown to them and us?
- What essential knowledge and skills must all students have to be successful now and later in life?
- How do we empower students to participate actively in the rigor of problem-solving, critical thinking, and creativity?

In designing the school improvement plan, additional questions will arise, some simple in nature and others more complex. What strategies will be used to monitor students' progress? In what ways will diverse learner needs be met? How will the attainment of goals be determined? These and any other questions must not be overlooked. This open, proactive approach will lead to a more comprehensive plan in which the needs of both students and teachers will be better served.

COMMUNICATE PRIORITIES AND PROGRESS

The process of arriving at goals for improved student learning and school effectiveness is not a simple task. However, communicating priorities, the final statement of goals to all stakeholders, is imperative. The school improvement plan is the vehicle that shares the goals and the action steps for achieving them in a single comprehensive document. Designating action steps to achieve goals communicates that they are attainable. The school improvement plan designates a timeline, assigns ownership and responsibility for monitoring action steps, and designates resources needed to achieve goals. Evaluating progress and communicating results are both critical in this process.

PRIORITIZING NEEDS: STUDENTS, COMMUNITY, AND SOCIETY

The needs of students cannot be completely separated into the categories of school, community, and societal needs. They are all interwoven and intersect. Schools were formed by and for society; society supports schools. Schools then, in turn, influence society with citizenship, education, and preparing students for the twenty-first-century workforce. Educators must work for the community that supports the school.

DECISION-MAKING THROUGH DATA

Decisions made by educational leaders must be carefully thought out and based on data and research. While prioritizing the needs of society as a whole, the community, school, and the students cannot be taken lightly. The ability of our school leaders to assess the needs of our diverse students is extremely important to how we make decisions necessary to make essential changes.

- What are the current needs of society, the community, and students?
- Do we have the data to support the needs?
- How do we know if needs are being met?
- As we make changes, are we following up to see what is working and what is not?
- Are we preparing our students for the twenty-first century?
- Have we considered our differing student and community populations (in terms of religion, morals, multiculturalism, language barriers, illiteracy, income, and achievement)?
- Have we thought about the school and community traditions?
- Does the current curriculum meet the needs of the students, school, community, and society?

As an educational leader, decisions about curriculum must be based on research. Before decisions are made it is very important to do the following:

- Review studies favoring a particular practice and also review research that contradicts those practices.
- Pay attention to the authors of the research. Look out for bias.
- Do actual research! Make decisions based not on feelings, but on what has been proven to work. This removes unnecessary "blame" from the

decision-maker and backs up the decision. State what is found in the research.

- Make decisions based on data and validated by research and sound education principles.

Student Performance Data

In the United States, we have become more and more standards driven. Local districts, states, and even the nation use performance data based on objectives or standards in specific subject and grade areas. There is a plethora of data regarding student achievement, gaps, strengths, and deficiencies.

Twenty-first-century classrooms are no longer textbook driven, but standards driven. These twenty-first-century classrooms are required to evolve to meet the needs of diverse modern students, guiding them to transfer knowledge and understanding into the community and the world. For student performance data to be useful to teachers and leaders, it must come from multiple data sources, be collected/analyzed/interpreted regularly over time, and provide feedback that educators can act upon.

Student performance data is not one or two standardized tests given at the end of the school year, but data from multiple sources/assessments collected regularly throughout the school year. This data should be interpreted regularly. What was learned? What was missing? What should be retaught in a different way? Based on the performance represented in this data, did the students meet the standards?

Much attention in current literature has been given to distinguishing between formal and informal assessment, as well as formative and summative assessment. Regardless of the term assigned, at the core of any assessment is providing feedback so that students know how to improve their understanding and produce high-quality work. It is a reciprocal process that benefits both the student and the teacher. Formative assessment is any method of providing feedback to students prior to completing a unit of instruction, that is, while there is still time to improve.

The common thread throughout the research on formative assessment is emphasis on gathering information on what students know and do not know and then providing feedback for improving. It is descriptive, timely, and ongoing. It is intended to help the student move to the next level of learning by identifying what the student already understands while offering suggestions for how to improve in areas not yet mastered.[5]

COMMUNITY DEMOGRAPHICS

Society and local community demographics influence schools. Schools have the responsibility and obligation to take hold of opportunities to improve the community and society. There are many societal and communal factors that influence schools, including the following:

- Parental Involvement
- Morals/Values
- Income/Poverty
- Family Structure
- Multiculturalism
- Religion
- Achievement
- Resources
- Language Barriers

The issue confronting today's classroom teachers is how to meet the needs of diverse learners in a standards-based environment. One way to confront this challenge head-on is with formative assessments (data) and through differentiating instruction as a means to improving learning for all students. In this context, as defined by Chapman and King (2005), "Differentiation is a philosophy that enables teachers to plan strategically in order to reach the needs of diverse learners today."[6]

Each community and school have their own identity, demographics, and barriers. It is important as educational leaders to get to know the culture and identity of the school(s) and community.

- Find out the strengths and weaknesses.
- Find ways to build not only on the weaknesses, but on the strengths as well.
- Look for ways to build up the students, faculty, community, and society.
- Use curriculum that lends itself to differentiation to meet the diverse needs of the learners.

SELECTING A MODEL FOR TWENTY-FIRST-CENTURY CURRICULUM

How might existing philosophies be interpreted in light of twenty-first-century learning? What does each have to offer in preparing students today for their future? A snapshot of how curriculum is viewed within the philosophies discussed is an entry point in guiding a school community through its deliberations in selecting the best-fit philosophy and model for continuous school improvement.

Essentialists approach the curriculum in a systematic and methodical order. Persisting in rigor and fidelity, they prepare students with essential knowledge and skills in reading, writing, mathematics, history, and English, and they ensure that students are ready to enter college. However, there is little, if any, room for diversity and the individual needs of students.

Reform efforts today also include tenets consistent with perennialism. This philosophy endorses the inclusion of more mathematics and science in the curriculum. The perennialists' learning environment mimics that of the essentialists: Classical subjects are right for everyone, so there is no need to be concerned about learners' interests and needs.

The progressivist environment encourages active participation among learners. Learners are leading. Learners are teaching each other. Learners are selecting content and learning activities. Students are collaborating; they are solving new and challenging problems. Courses, skills, and the learning environment are organized to promote lifelong learning, successful adult work, and contributing citizenship.

The reconstructionist curriculum combines study with social action. The purpose of what is taught is to raise students' conscientiousness of major problems in society. The goal is to prepare students to contribute to ameliorating social problems.

Equipped with the knowledge of these existing philosophies, is it possible for a school to define its own philosophy? In her discussion of the disciplines, Heidi Hayes Jacobs (2010) boldly proclaims, "A Curriculum 21 review team should challenge prevailing practices with vigorous intellectual, rational, and forward thinking."[7] This boldness, however, is not limited to a single team. It is part of a compelling context in which all school personnel must approach curriculum. It is the only way to equip students in their learning environment with the knowledge and skills to adapt in a changing twenty-first-century world.

While several well-known curriculum models have been studied and utilized by curriculum developers, the Parallel Curriculum Model proposed by Tomlinson and Parrish (2010) offers a framework consisting of four interrelated parallels, each referred to as a curriculum: Core, Connections, Practice, and Identity. Each parallel has components that align with the other.[8] The comprehensive framework allows school leaders and teachers to design, evaluate, and revise existing curriculum. School accountability, twenty-first-century knowledge and skills, learners' needs, the art and science of teaching—all are included and integrated in this model.

The Core Curriculum and Curriculum of Connections combine major concepts of content areas by connecting overarching concepts within and across disciplines. The Curriculum of Practice allows students to gain competency as problem-solvers, producers, or practitioners in a field. The Curriculum of Identity allows students to develop their interests, improve strengths, and develop by participating in fields and projects that support personal growth.

The Parallel Curriculum Model supports leadership through the rigor and relevance framework developed by the International Center for Leadership in Education. The Application Model, created by Willard Daggett, is characterized by the coexistence of high levels of knowledge and application. School leaders, teachers, and students share this attribute.[9] Evaluating curriculum in this environment requires widening the lens, probing deep to find innovative and new ways for improving the instructional program and student learning. Synthesizing important evaluation principles might also help ignite new energy in the process of curriculum evaluation.

GUIDING PRINCIPLES FOR EVALUATING CURRICULUM

School leaders and practitioners continue to seek ways to effectively review, evaluate, and update curriculum driven by well-founded principles of curriculum planning and development. This ongoing process necessitates gathering data, including, but not limited to, student performance, stakeholder perception, classroom observations, and course and program portfolios.

Multiple questions are included in the evaluation process. What are we doing? Is our program of studies consistent with what we know about designing a rich, rigorous, and relevant curriculum? Are courses and support programs serving the needs of all students? Is the curriculum taking into account the long-term needs of students? Is what we are doing consistent with what we now know about learning and teaching? Is technology used consistently to support ongoing learning and to develop skills connected to the workplace? Is the curriculum aligned with the needs of society, both locally and globally? How is the curriculum nurturing well-rounded individuals?

Reflecting and making decisions continuously is integral to curriculum evaluation. The well-known CIPP model suggests four types of evaluation: context, input, process, and product.[10] Though novel, one critical-thinking approach is to begin by categorizing each type of evaluation by the guiding principles of curriculum planning and evaluation with which educators are most familiar: scope, relevance, balance, integration, sequence, continuity, articulation, and transferability.

Input Evaluation: What procedural designs and educational strategies will most likely achieve desired results?

- **Balance:** Is the overall school structure leading to the achievement of goals and objectives? How is each being addressed: needs of society vs. needs of learner; innovation vs. tradition; needs of average student vs. needs of accelerated student? Is the curriculum limiting or expanding learning?
- **Integration:** Is there a blending of themes across multiple subject areas? Are performance tasks designed to incorporate learning across disciplines? How and by whom are components of performance tasks being assessed?
- **Sequence:** Are essential topics within courses appropriately placed throughout the year? Are courses placed at the appropriate grade levels to ensure higher development of critical-thinking and problem-solving skills from one grade level to the next? Have maturation, experiential background of learners, and usefulness and difficulty of subject matter been considered?

Context Evaluation: The basic questions to be asked include what needs to be done, how can assets and opportunities be identified, and how will problems be assessed. These questions may be paired with guiding principles, scope, and relevance.

- **Scope:** Does the curriculum reflect essential and supporting content, activities, and learning experiences to promote academic success in all disciplines?
- **Relevance:** Does instruction in all courses consistently take into account students' interests and experiences? Is the curriculum preparing students for their next level of learning? Is the rigor of the curriculum preparing students for college and the workplace?

Process Evaluation: This is the ongoing implementation phase of curriculum evaluation. The major questions are is what is supposed to be happening taking place, is there ongoing documentation of the process, is substantive feedback being provided, and what adjustments or revisions are needed?

- **Articulation:** Are curriculum goals clearly communicated to all stakeholders? Are teachers working horizontally within subject areas to ensure consistency in grade-level expectations? Is vertical alignment consistently implemented to achieve learning goals as students move from one grade level to the next?
- **Continuity:** Is there planned repetition of skills throughout the curriculum, each time at an increased level of complexity? Is scaffolding consistently

applied in the spiral curriculum as students encounter new concepts, skills, and knowledge?

Product Evaluation: Did the curriculum succeed? Can the merit, worth, and significance of the curriculum be assessed? Are the outcomes measurable? Product evaluation may be referred to as recycling decisions. The curriculum principle closely associated with product evaluation is transferability.

• **Transferability:** Is the learning taking place in the classroom applicable outside of school? Will the skills emphasized provide a successful tomorrow for today's students?

Curriculum evaluation is intended to determine if school goals and learning objectives are being met. The guiding principles of curriculum evaluation are intended to help school leaders, curriculum teams, and teachers make judgments for improving learning for all students. This process involves studying the research, collecting and analyzing relevant school data, working as a team, and being attentive to the needs of students, the school community, and society. As this ongoing evaluation process evolves, new goals are set and the plan for monitoring and evaluating progress is revised.

PEDAGOGY AND TWENTY-FIRST-CENTURY LEARNER NEEDS

To meet twenty-first-century learner needs, teachers must play an active role in evaluating their curriculum. Curriculum alignment, integration, and uniformity of what is taught to what is tested provides needed direction and feedback for teachers. Teachers becoming involved in curriculum evaluation, the school's mission, and grade-level goals create a sense of "buy-in," which in turn provides an understanding of the interconnected components and the "how" and "why" of decision-making.

In our era of high-stakes testing and standardization, alignment of curriculum standards and assessments has gained importance locally, at the district level, statewide, and nationwide. This alignment of the curriculum is a better practice than preparing students to take tests. When aligning, evaluating, and developing curriculum to meet learner needs, it is important to examine across grade levels and through each grade level to ensure consistencies throughout.

Although the curriculum and assessments must be evaluated and aligned to ensure consistent building blocks and goals throughout levels, the diverse needs of student learners must be examined. The psychologist Lev Vygotsky

(1978) tells us that students learn when they are working in their zone of proximal development.[11] The zone of proximal development includes the variety of challenges in which learning takes place, because the task is neither too hard nor too easy.

Educators must note that a one-size-fits-all model is unlikely to meet the needs of all learners in a specific classroom. There are many methods to instructing and educating students. Differentiation of instruction is an approach that honors differences in learning and the interests and needs of students, and responds accordingly. With a high-quality curriculum, and keeping students' abilities and differences in mind, differentiation allows students to meet their potential.

A twenty-first-century classroom must keep in mind the importance of teaching twenty-first-century skills to prepare our students to be successful after formal schooling. Important skills for twenty-first-century classrooms should include, but not be limited to, problem-solving, critical thinking, collaborative partnerships, communication, technology, and creativity. Learning is a process. Students learn and grow by making mistakes and taking chances. Learning environments should be a safe and secure place to foster academic and social growth.

ALIGNING CONTENT STANDARDS AND ASSESSMENT

Content standards, or expectations for learners and what students should know and be able to do, are where curriculum evaluation starts. How will we know students have met the standards? The answer to this question depends on careful and deliberate planning. Planning means infusing life into the standards by incorporating sound principles of assessment to determine what students know and can do from participating in a variety of learning opportunities.

These learning opportunities are the outcome of unit assessment planning. Unit plans for major content in all courses include an alignment of content standards, learning objectives, and assessments, both formative and summative. The state or district typically promulgates content standards. Most learning objectives are readily extracted from state content standards; others are stated in the context of a school's improvement goals. Assessment encompasses all the procedures and processes used to gather information about student progress during instruction and at the end of a unit of instruction, grading period, semester, or year.

The purpose of evaluating curriculum is the same as the purpose of evaluating instruction: to know if what we are doing is helping students learn. Based on this judgment, changes for improvement will be planned, implemented, and monitored. Throughout this cyclic process the focus areas of maximum learning and achievement and instruction and assessment cannot be thought of independently; they are a marriage.

UNIT ALIGNMENT WITH STANDARDS, OBJECTIVES, AND ASSESSMENTS

Evaluating curriculum is generally understood as assessing programs, processes, and utilization of resources. To facilitate the ongoing evaluation of the overall instructional program, using common tools is recommended. One such tool is the unit assessment plan. The unit assessment plan demonstrates the alignment of standards, objectives, and assessments for major unit topics in subjects throughout the curriculum. The elements represented in the unit assessment plan include:

a. **Unit Identification:** Subject Area, Course Name, Grade Level, Title of Unit
b. **Academic Standards:** Statement of the state's academic standards related to the unit topic and the citation code for each of these standards
c. **Learning Objectives:** Statements of learning objectives spanning multiple levels of thinking and doing, each aligned with the intent of one or more standards related to the unit topic
d. **Formative Assessments:** A variety of formative assessments are selected or designed to monitor progress during instruction and to provide feedback for improving.
e. **Formal Classroom Assessments:** Formal assessments are aligned with objectives. The assessments include essential and important course content, span simple to complex levels of thinking and application, and focus on performance skills specified in the standards or identified in school improvement goals. Formal assessments, including teacher-made and standardized assessments, are used to determine how well students have met the standards.

Caution! A student's score on a standardized test does not represent everything a student knows in a content area. Topics on a standardized test may not yet have been taught when the test is administered. Well-designed local and district assessments, aligned with standards and objectives, are more likely to indicate which objectives have been met and which have not been met by each student. The alignment of expectations for learning with appropriate assessments will enhance validity, thus increasing the prospect of making better decisions throughout curriculum planning and evaluation.

ALIGNING INSTRUCTIONAL RESOURCES WITH LEARNING STANDARDS/OBJECTIVES

Learning standards, content standards, objectives, and expectations, all mentioned previously, drive the instructional resources and curriculum. Aligning instructional resources and curriculum to learning standards and activities, and then later in the process to assessment and feedback, is key to success. For students to meet the standards/goals set forth, proper alignment must occur throughout.

What exactly is alignment? Do the materials, activities, and resources "match up" with what is being tested? Do these tests (assessments) prove that students are meeting standards/goals? Research has found that oftentimes this is not the case. In fact, learning activities do not always match with assessments, and assessments do not always match with standards and objectives. This is detrimental to students. For students to meet learning goals, it is vital that they be taught what is expected of them.

Gathering feedback is another important feature of alignment. Feedback can be gathered formally or informally through a variety of resources. This is done throughout the process of gathering resources and planning the curriculum, teaching and learning, reviewing standards and assessments, and working with students and teachers. This is a constant cycle. What is working? What is not working? Do our learning goals, activities, and assessments allow students the opportunity to meet their goals?

Alignment is extremely important. Teachers may be outstanding, but if their teaching is not aligned to state standards or assessments, their teaching is unproductive. In an age of educational accountability, this alignment is crucial to student success.

CHAPTER SUMMARY

In this chapter, curriculum evaluation has been presented as an ongoing review of the systems and practices of a school or school district to determine the quality of the overall impact of a school's curriculum on student achievement. This approach described the process as robust, examining all critical aspects of school to determine what is working well, what needs changing, what goals have been met, and what new goals and processes should be in place to improve maximal student learning and success. This understanding and approach to curriculum evaluation expressed the importance of including school stakeholders in the process, particularly teachers.

As described in this chapter, curriculum evaluation examines the alignment of a school's philosophical beliefs with its goals and processes. It is grounded in well-known and sound principles of evaluation that work side by side with twenty-first-century endeavors to bring rigor and relevance to the forefront in today's schools. An evaluation of curriculum necessitates responding to today's learner needs while equipping students with knowledge and skills that will endure five, ten, twenty, and even forty years from now.

Analyzing existing data is integral to making decisions about the value of a school's current program. Analyzing, interpreting, and using data gives rise to specific and meaningful goals that can help eliminate gaps in student performance or fulfill needs uncovered when evaluating a school's academic program. Then the process of aligning instruction and assessment practices with goals, standards, and resources begins anew, forming the backbone of all school improvement efforts and framing the need for ongoing curriculum evaluation.

NOTES

1. Kenneth T. Henson, *Curriculum Planning: Integrating Multiculturalism, Constructivism, and Education Reform* (Long Grove, IL: Waveland Press, 2015), 122.

2. Ibid.

3. Ralph W. Tyler, *Basic Principles of Curriculum and Instruction* (Chicago: University of Chicago Press, 1971), 53.

4. Jay McTighe and Grant Wiggins, *Essential Questions: Opening Doors to Student Understanding* (Alexandria, VA: ASCD, 2013), 82.

5. W. J. Popham, *Transformative Assessment in Action: An Inside Look at Applying the Process* (Alexandria, VA: ASCD, 2011).

6. Carolyn Chapman and Rita King, *Differentiated Assessment Strategies: One Tool Doesn't Fit All* (Thousand Oaks, CA: Corwin Press, 2005), xxii.

7. Heidi Hayes Jacobs, *Curriculum 21: Essential Education for a Changing World* (Alexandria, VA: ASCD, 2010), 32.

8. Carol A. Tomlinson and William Parrish Jr., "21st Century Skills and the Parallel Curriculum Model," Presentation at the National Association for Gifted Children, Atlanta, GA, November 14, 2010.

9. Richard D. Jones, *Rigor and Relevance Handbook* (Rexford, NY: International Center for Leadership in Education, Inc., 2010), http://www.doe.in.gov/sites/default/files/cte/ncteb-rigorrev.pdf.

10. G. Zhang, N. Zeller, R. Griffith, D. Metcalf, J. Williams, C. Shea, and K. Misulis, "Using the Context, Input, Process, and Product Evaluation Model (CIPP) as a Comprehensive Framework to Guide the Planning, Implementation, and Assessment of Service-Learning Programs," *Journal of Higher Education Outreach and Engagement* 15, no. 4 (2011): 57–84, http://files.eric.ed.gov/ fulltext/EJ957107.pdf.

11. Lev Vygotsky, *Mind in Society: The Development of Higher Psychological Processes* (Cambridge, MA: Harvard University Press, 1978).

Chapter 6

Organizing the Learning Environment

Bertha Myers, EdS, and Ronald J. Dore', EdS

As teachers and school administrators quickly learn, safety and respect in any school setting provides for the management of good behavior and ensures a successful school year. A well-managed classroom is an environment in which administrators, teachers, and students know that their responsibility is to ensure that effective teaching and learning take place. In order for this to happen, mutual respect from all school personnel must be expected.

Good behavior usually results in better student achievement. Students, therefore, must be provided an environment that is conducive to good behavior, which, in turn, is conducive to teaching and learning. Such an environment enhances students' personal growth and responsible citizenship.

Learning takes place best when students feel safe, cared for, and valued. Moreover, students must be engaged in activities that challenge them but do not overwhelm them. When students work hard, get regular feedback from their teachers, and behave well with little to no disruptions, they progress at their pace and enjoy the feeling of success each day they enter the classroom. In short, they feel good about themselves for their achievement, thereby allowing their self-esteem to develop in a positive manner.

The culture of the school plays an important role. Implementation of a diverse school plan helps to assure the creation of a culture in which all feel welcomed and valued. It is not enough for only teachers and students to feel safe and respected; all staff members, parents, visitors, and community members must also feel safe and respected. School culture and climate speak louder than any poster or policies on the walls.

SCHOOL CULTURE

In general, school culture refers to the beliefs, attitudes, and perceptions that influence every aspect of how a school functions. Moreover, the term encompasses issues such as the physical and emotional safety of students. As a regular daily routine, safety and respect should be modeled and encouraged. School policies should include elements that advocate respect among students, teachers, administrators, and staff.

It is the writers' belief that students play an active role in the creation of behavior guidelines. In addition to schoolwide and individual classroom expectations, the behavior guidelines should include the following:

- High expectations for all students and the message that all students can succeed academically
- Emotional and academic support for all students
- Empathy and positive interactions for all stakeholders
- Behavior guidelines and expectations prominently displayed
- Praise and encouragement frequently provided
- Regular and routine celebration and recognition of success of students and staff
- Incentives to motivate and increase appropriate behaviors provided[1]

The culture of each classroom should be one that is essentially positive. Students in such classrooms are actively engaged in learning activities, routinely cooperate with their teachers, and collaborate with their peers. Teachers are fair and consistent in their treatment and expectations of each child. When the culture of the classroom creates an atmosphere in which the students feel safe and secure and have a strong sense of self-worth, the teacher's instructional goals/objectives are usually met.

SCHOOL SAFETY

With the changing dynamics of society, school administrators and teachers must work diligently to create and maintain a safe and secure environment. This involves continuous monitoring and making appropriate adjustments. There are many federal, state, and local mandates that impact policies and procedures. One of the more important areas requiring regular monitoring is on-campus traffic. In addition to staff traffic and parking needs, it is important to also monitor the busses and traffic of parents dropping off and picking up their students.

SCHOOL TRAFFIC CONTROL

Not all elementary or middle schools are designed with an excess of parking areas. With increasing levels of parental involvement, greater numbers of parents are attending school events. Consideration needs to be taken to ensure a safe, conducive area for all to park. It may mean that faculty parking is reassigned during these times. If more parking space is needed, a procedure to accommodate additional visitors must be in the initial planning phase of any event.

To achieve an orderly and safe flow of traffic in school areas, personnel must treat traffic situations in a diligent and consistent manner. Parents must be cognizant of the established ways of dropping off their children on campus. Schools must provide parents information regarding drop-off and pick-up times. Parents and visitors must be made aware of appropriate parking spaces. Students driving on campus should be required to register their vehicles with the school office.

CRISIS PLANS

A crisis plan is a vital part of a school's emergency preparedness program. As mentioned earlier, each school's success is dependent upon the safety of its students. It is of utmost importance that every school create and implement a crisis plan that is tailored to its unique and specific needs. Every school's crisis plan is considered an integral part of its management plan. It is also important that the elements of the crisis plan are communicated and understood by the school staff, students, and parents. Regular practice and drills involving the school crisis team, students, and the entire staff are a necessity. Everyone needs to be fully aware of every possible scenario and of the appropriate actions to be taken for each scenario. A well-designed plan that is properly executed may save the life of a student and/or a school staff member.

Influenced by recent events reported in the media, school officials have reexamined and refined their school crisis plans. They recognize the importance of having in place school crisis plans and trained personnel whose purpose and goals are to reduce, if not eliminate, danger to students and staff. The community expects schools to not only deal with any crisis, but also prevent most. Many define crisis plans as those action steps needed to be put into place at the onset of critical situations. Crisis plans need to take into account steps, including in-house procedures and routines that prevent a crisis from occurring. These prevention steps can be part of plans in areas such as general traffic control, student movement throughout the day, visitors' procedures, and expectations of teachers and staff.

A school building safety manual may be provided to each school in the district, and site-based rules/regulations should be established as well.

- The principal or site administrator (in the absence of the principal) determines the level of the emergency response needed.
- All school personnel are informed of the security and response procedures.
- An evaluation is conducted if an incident occurs.
- The principal serves as the School Crisis or Facility Coordinator along with his/her designees.
- The administrative designees have the authority to search any classroom, employee, or student if a school rule or board policy has been violated. However, reasonable grounds to suspect that the search would reveal evidence that the individual has violated the law, school rule, or school board policy must be established. The search is to be conducted in a manner that is reasonably related to the purpose of the search and not be excessively intrusive in retrospect to age or sex of the individual and the nature of the suspected offense.
- If a physical confrontation occurs on campus during extracurricular activities, a thorough investigation of the incident needs to be conducted.
- To encourage learning and ensure safety, a school may adopt a Positive Behavior Incentive Support (PBIS) program. An emphasis on teaching and modeling appropriate behavior, recognizing and rewarding appropriate behavior, and consequences for inappropriate behaviors is the goal of the program.
- Security cameras may be installed in different areas of the school to address problems with break-ins, robberies, or vandalizing of the school.[2]

Many districts encourage or require schools to follow a given template or policy for these action steps. Lines of communication such as phone trees, a text messaging system, or email distribution lists need to be established well before any crisis situation ever occurs. A common vocabulary should be agreed upon in the event of multiple agencies being involved.

Even though districts may provide templates for plans, they should never be created or developed by a select few. Committees need to include administrators, teachers, staff, community support personnel, parents, and students, and most importantly, emergency responders such as state and local police, fire departments, and emergency medical personnel. These emergency responders need to be involved in all phases of the creation of a school crisis plan and its oversight, as well as be fully involved in all emergency drills.

Plans need to assure the safety of students, teachers, staff, and visitors. Procedures must exist that address a variety of scenarios. Well-developed emergency policies and school crisis plans contain the following components:

- Roles and responsibilities of all designees and alternates along with a description of each person's duties and responsibilities for each emergency scenario
- Procedures/action steps that include but are not limited to the following:
  - A school lockdown process should be in place for times when, for various reasons, students and staff are required to evacuate hallways and large gathering areas and either remain in or move to individual classrooms.
  - Lockdown procedures are utilized when administrators become aware of a situation that may endanger students.
  - Teachers and staff members are to respond to the lockdown procedures as listed in the school crisis response plan.
  - No one should leave the room until a signal is given that the situation is clear.
  - All movement needs to be stopped, and all doors locked until the principal or law enforcement gives the signal that all is clear.
  - Lockdown alerts include, but are not limited to, weapons on campus, gangs/intruders, natural disasters, riots, trespassing, attempted kidnappings, deaths on campus, hostage situations, suicides, suicide attempts, rapes, homicides, and medical emergencies. Precautions must be taken, and the crisis prevention handbook must be adhered to in all instances.
- Procedures for when an intruder is on campus: If an intruder is on campus, the school's faculty, staff, or student(s) must report this immediately to the principal to take protective actions. Some of the suggested measures are as follows:
  - Lock all doors, if in a classroom.
  - Tell the students to remain calm and give an accurate description of the person(s) if possible, such as clothing the intruder is wearing, the intruder's height, weight, sex, and any other physical characteristics, the weapon if known, and the location of the intruder.
  - Lock all windows and close all blinds.
  - Turn off all lights and audio equipment.
  - Stay out of any open areas and be as quiet as possible.
  - Look for a safe and secure hiding place if in an open area.
  - If the need to escape arises, run in a zigzag manner.
  - "Play dead" by assuming a prone position if unable to hide and the intruder is causing injury or death.

- Fight back (only as a last resort) if in close proximity to the intruder.
- Obey all commands and assist anyone who needs help.[3]
- Evacuation plans for immediate and swift evacuation of the school building. It is important to note that evacuation plans may involve transportation to areas and/or buildings where students can congregate safely away from any danger zone. These evacuation plans must address any concerns regarding traffic flow and its impact on the ability of emergency vehicles to access the school.
- Designation of areas and procedures which allow for parents to be reunited with their children
- Severe weather procedures, which are appropriate for weather conditions that may threaten the safety of students and staff
- District- and building-level emergency codes, which serve to inform staff members of the type of threat and of the appropriate actions of staff
- Debriefing procedures so that appropriate information can be shared with the staff and public while an emergency situation unfolds. Debriefing by the school's emergency response team and community emergency responders should take place as soon as possible in order to review the processes and procedures followed during the emergency. The purpose of the debriefing is to evaluate the quality and appropriateness of the responses and to identify and address areas of concern.

SAFE ENVIRONMENT: FIRE DRILL/LAW ENFORCEMENT

Fire drills are viewed as routine procedures in school. Practicing the procedures on a regular basis increases the success of the drill. Some safety tips for fire drills are as follows:

- Hold fire drills periodically while school is in session.
- Inspect all exits to ensure they are working properly and are unblocked.
- Sound the drill alarm and make sure all faculty, staff, and students recognize the sound of the alarm and know what to do when it sounds.
- Provide maps to identify ways out of the school building.
- Have everyone participate on the day of the fire drill.
- Assist any student who needs help with exiting the building (be certain to establish evacuation plans for all students with physical disabilities that may prevent or hinder their efforts to swiftly evacuate the building).
- Make sure everyone exits the building in a quick and orderly manner.
- Reenter the school when safety personnel state that it is safe to reenter.
- Make sure everyone is accounted for at all times.[4] (This holds true for any emergency situation. Teachers must be assigned specific areas where

their students are to gather and are required to take attendance and follow procedures to report any missing students immediately.)

Schools should ask for and rely on any assistance from fire department and law enforcement personnel. Many fire departments have fire drills at schools in which all students, teachers, and staff are to evacuate the premises in a safe, orderly, and timely manner. They may provide information to assist with safety improvements.

Law enforcement plays a significant role at a school. Schools, at times, may be used as training facilities. For example, when schools are not in session, officers often use schools as simulated-emergency practice areas to assess the validity of any plans and procedures they may develop that address crisis situations in schools. Law enforcement personnel may practice tactical operations to secure the school. Such exercises help law enforcement agencies to gather information to provide better security in all schools in the district.

It is very common for schools to have School Resource Officers (SROs) assigned to monitor and provide security during the school day as well as during extracurricular events. SROs are specifically trained law enforcement officers who are responsible for providing security services at schools. The school's resource officer is a designee of law enforcement and follows the chain of command as designated by his/her superiors. Indicated below are some of the officer's duties. Please note that this is not an all-inclusive list of an SRO's responsibilities:

- Serve as liaison between the police department and the school
- Assist with crisis planning at school
- Build positive relationships with students
- Deter misconduct through prevention and intervention
- Attend and participate in school functions

USE OF SCHOOL FACILITY

A school is viewed as a very important part of any community. The school often serves as the central gathering place of the community. It is seen as a place where parents can watch and enjoy their children at athletic, academic, musical, and celebratory events. The public considers its school as a place of security, where children are prepared academically and emotionally to become successful, contributing members of society.

Some organizations, especially those that serve the community, appreciate the fact that the building is available for use by community organizations.

Usually, with the permission of the school board, the school facility can be used for the purposes listed below whenever the school is not in session:

- Any branch of education meeting
- Social, civic, and recreational meetings
- Polling place for elections
- Place for civic forums and community centers
- Military gatherings with family and friends prior to military deployment
- Law enforcement practice sessions

The district often adopts usage fees and proof of insurance to cover the costs of electricity, maintenance, custodial services, and any other expenses associated with the requested use. Often it is required that a school staff member be present during the event. It must be noted that tobacco, alcoholic beverages, and unlawful drugs are never to be distributed, consumed, promoted, or possessed at any time on school grounds.

COLLABORATIVE PLANNING

Prior to the beginning of each school year, the school's principal and designees should meet with the entire faculty and staff to discuss classes to be taught, to provide each teacher his/her classroom schedule, and to discuss schoolwide policies. The meeting should allow for collaborative ideas whose focus is to build and maintain strong relationships between administrators and staff. One of the building blocks of these relationships involves providing teachers with opportunities to expand and refine their instructional knowledge and skills through professional development.

One of the desired relationships includes the concept of distributed leadership, in which teachers are expected to play decisive roles in contributing to the solutions of any problems or concerns that may arise during the academic year. Distributive leadership strengthens teacher involvement in the functioning of the school by providing input that assists in the decision-making process.

With increased emphasis on accountability, faculty meetings need to be focused and meaningful while addressing the school's needs. Grade-level meetings provide opportunities for the administrative team to both identify and target areas of concern. Newly implemented improvement strategies should be continuously monitored so that changes and adjustments can be made to ensure future success. Last but not least, areas where improvements and successes have been made should be celebrated.

It is extremely important that schools reach out to parents and caregivers to form and strengthen partnerships that work to provide students all of the educational and emotional support they may need to become lifelong learners and hold successful careers. Business and school partnerships play a similar role and allow schools and businesses the opportunity to work together to provide students with experiences beyond the regular curriculum. School/business partnerships help to create activities and experiences that motivate students to enjoy their time in school, raise their expectations, and strive to become college, career, and citizen-ready. The advantages of school/business partnerships are many. Some of them are listed below:

- Increase school pride among faculty, staff, and students
- Enrich the school by having business personnel visit the classrooms
- Enhance the business's image throughout the community
- Develop possible future employees
- Emphasize the importance of education
- Encourage participation from stakeholders while reinforcing that education is top priority
- Gain appreciation for the challenges and rewards of teaching
- Provide students the opportunity to expand career awareness
- Inspire students to set goals for themselves
- Provide real-world application of skills
- Provide role models to emulate
- Bring financial resources to schools to provide quality education[5]

FINANCIAL STATUS/SCHOOL BUDGETING/ SITE-BASED MANAGING

Central office personnel may include district supervisors and other certified personnel who are trained in accounting, business, taxation, etc. These personnel are responsible for evaluating all of the district's purchase orders and all money that is collected by the district as well as by individual school buildings. There are, however, designated individuals in each school building who are responsible for all monetary transactions occurring within an individual school. Their duties and responsibilities are to review all purchase orders, pay invoices, count petty cash, and monitor the cash flow.

In order to improve accuracy and limit possible fraud, a check-and-balance system should be established in the school. The building principal holds ultimate responsibility for the proper maintenance of all school financial records and the accounts being in compliance with all monetary policies. This is always the case even though others may be designated by the principal to oversee the school's finances. Schools are nonprofit organizations but many times have a significant amount of money on hand. Fund-raisers, in-house school activities, and sporting events are just some of the examples of events requiring personnel to follow written financial procedures.

Within a school district, individual schools are required to pay monthly school-related bills as well as maintain operating capital for clubs and athletic departments. Regular audits are conducted for accountability purposes. For example, site-based management is a system in which the central office personnel delegate the decision-making process to the individual schools. That is, they will be putting more responsibility on the school and allowing the educational institution to solve its own problems without any assistance from the central office.

The principal is usually the site manager and is therefore responsible for the decision-making process of the school. The principal, however, is not the sole authority figure in the school. Teachers play a fiscal role in the school when they routinely collect fees from students to purchase resources for the classroom.

In short, teachers and school administrators confer with each other to reach decisions regarding the running of the school. However, it is important to note that there are some pitfalls to the approach of site-based decision-making. For example, most of these schools rarely have the right resources to provide training for the site-based members, thereby negatively affecting the quality of their financial decisions.[6]

SCHEDULING PROCESS

Creating a master schedule is so much more than aligning courses to teaching assignments. Consideration must be given to the layout of the facility, student movement, lunch schedules, singletons and doubletons (classes that occur only once or twice during the day), number of students and course sections, sharing teachers at two or more separate school locations, teacher certification areas, teacher contracts, and availability of resources.

Preparation for scheduling begins many months before the actual schedule is created. An administrative team or designee begins by collecting information including expected student counts in each course in each grade level, the number of teachers needed based on the counts, and availability of rooms. One of the first tasks in the scheduling process is to gather information regarding accommodations, assignment of aides, level of inclusion for each student, and teaching assignments of the special education staff.

Most schools have computer software that stores information on every special needs student. It is extremely important to gather and accurately record this information. A careful review of this information should be undertaken in order to ensure that schedules of special needs students faithfully meet the educational requirements stated in each special needs student's Individual Educational Plan (IEP). Spreadsheets make this task less cumbersome by allowing the scheduler to view the entire student academic profile.

Effective scheduling affects the overall atmosphere and functioning of a school. A well-designed master schedule has a positive impact on school safety. It will also provide teachers with the time to collaborate in the design of learning activities and assessments, make adjustments to the curricula, and monitor student academic performance. Teachers can also use this planning time for professional development as well as to measure the effectiveness of their lessons.

The principal is responsible for seeing that the master schedule provides for an efficient use of time and staff. She has the responsibility to oversee teachers' schedules and make certain that no conflicts exist between courses that may prevent students from taking any course or courses they may need to advance to the next level. She must also ensure that teaching assignments accurately match every teacher's qualifications and certification area.

In secondary schools where there may be a variety of high school diploma types and qualifications, the master schedule is driven by course requests made by students and by the type of diploma they seek to achieve. Every effort should be made to offer a sufficient number of classes to meet all students' requests and needs. In elementary and middle school settings, it is important to allocate time for disciplines other than the four core subjects, such as computer technology, library science, enrichment/tutorial classes, woodworking, etc.

CLASSROOM RESOURCES: STRATEGIC PLAN

Strategic planning is an ongoing process and an integral element that supports the successful functioning of a school organization. Strategic planning guides a school organization forward. It is proactive and its purpose is to help an organization reach its goals. It is important to note that an organization, upon achieving its desired goals, cannot curtail the strategic planning process. An organization without a strategic plan becomes an entity that invites stagnation.

A well-designed and meaningful strategic plan articulates a shared vision, mission, and school goals. An effective strategic plan encourages and considers input from the entire school staff. It is well thought out and executed, and shared with school personnel. The plan is accepted by all. Everyone takes ownership of the plan and actively works to achieve the established goals and objectives.

A well-implemented strategic plan requires cooperation and collaboration among both instructional and noninstructional staff. In summary, strategic planning provides a framework for the success of a school organization. Strategic planning is an important element and plays a major role in the creation of a school's vision and mission statement.[7]

A vision statement implies change. Creating a vision statement involves an analysis of data collected over at least a three-year period. These data represent the current state of the school regarding academic performance, teaching and learning, expectations, student discipline, and the perceptions of students, parents, and staff regarding various aspects of how the school functions.

The school vision team uses input from all stakeholders. Their input compares what they know is the current state of the school to what they would like the school to become. This comparison forms the foundation upon which the school vision is built.

The resultant vision statement serves to set the direction, goals, and objectives of the organization. Specifically, to create a school vision statement, stakeholders should consider the following data. What follows is a partial list of data sources, provided here as an example of the data that represent the current state of a school organization:

- Daily staff attendance
- Daily student attendance
- Staff retention rates
- Student academic performance
- Student behavior
- Curricula
- Teacher effectiveness
- Perceptions of students, parents, and staff regarding the functioning and quality of school programs

The mission statement is a plan that describes the actions the school will take to achieve its vision. The mission statement has to align with the vision statement. The school vision and mission statements both drive the school's strategic plan. Key terms and concepts must be blended in both the vision and mission statements, and both must be fully understood by school personnel, students, and stakeholders.[8]

PROFESSIONAL DEVELOPMENT/
CONTINUING EDUCATION

Educators, like other professionals in areas such as law, medicine, engineering, and scientific research, have a responsibility and, in some professions, a legal mandate to participate in professional development/continuing education activities in order to refresh, further develop, or refine their professional knowledge and skills. Educators must regularly participate in continuing education activities that will help to keep them current with the latest changes in best practices, education law, and learning standards and assessments.

In addition to addressing their particular professional needs in their respective content area(s), professional development/continuing education topics may be chosen for them by their supervisors. For example, teachers who are members of the school improvement team, school vision team, or strategic planning team are often required to attend training sessions that are designed to address the specific knowledge and skills relating to their responsibilities as team members. It is also very common for the principal and individual teachers to work together to design an individualized professional development plan that addresses areas that the principal deems necessary to improve teacher effectiveness.

For example, during the course of the academic year, the principal may have observed during classroom visits that a teacher's classroom management techniques require refinement, or the teacher's questioning techniques need improvement. These are but two examples of how a leader would use classroom observations and teacher evaluations to drive professional development plans.

The educational leader may create goals that might target, for example, improving schoolwide reading comprehension skills. He may decide to require the entire teaching staff to participate in professional development content such as reading across the curriculum. Professional development activities address an almost limitless variety of topics and content. An effective educational leader will tailor individual professional development plans to provide for the professional growth of individual teachers as well as developing schoolwide plans for the entire teaching staff. All of these plans are based on the principal's observations and analysis of academic, demographic, process, and perception data.

What follows are but a few examples of the professional development topics available today. This list is by no means representative of all the content that is currently available.

- Data Collection and Analysis
- Instructional Strategies
- Cooperative/Collaborative Strategies
- Professional Learning Communities
- Ethical Issues
- Behavior Management/Interventions
- Specific Curriculum/Updates
- New Teacher Orientation
- Technology Skills and the Integration of Technology with Classroom Instruction
- Individualized Education Plans
- Rights of Students and Parents of Special Needs Students
- Instructional Strategies for Teachers of Special Needs Students

CHAPTER SUMMARY

In this chapter one can see that organizing the learning environment is not by any means a simple process. An effective learning environment provides an organization with the tools and processes it needs to function at high levels of efficiency and facilitates teaching and learning. Organizing the learning environment involves multifaceted implementation of

- a school culture and climate that supports cooperation, collaboration, and high expectations of student performance;
- school safety plans and procedures to create and maintain a safe and secure atmosphere that is conducive to teaching and learning;
- school leadership that is characterized by cooperation and collaboration;
- the ability of the school community to use school facilities, which in turn creates and nurtures positive relationships that benefit both school and community;
- procedures that include safeguards for the proper handling of school-level finances;
- the ability to create a master schedule that efficiently uses available instructional time and school facilities and effectively creates teaching and duty assignments that match teachers' experience, qualifications, and certifications; and
- professional development and continuing education plans and activities that are data driven and based on building-level goals and classroom observations.

An educational leader who includes and implements the suggestions made in this chapter will discover that oversight characterized by diligence and patience will create a school in which students, parents, and staff all work together to provide students a world-class educational experience that will lead to academic and career success.

NOTES

1. Marie Amaro, "What Does It Mean to Have High Expectations for Your Students," (2016), https://thehighlyeffectiveteacher.com/what-does-it-mean-to-have-high-expectations-for-your-students/.

2. "Student/Parent Handbook," (2017–2018), St. Martin Parish School System, www.saintmartinschools.org.

3. "Active Shooter, How to Respond," (2008), U.S. Dept. of Homeland Security, cfsteam@hq.dhs.gov.www.dhs.gov.

4. "School Safety Tips," (2016), National Fire Protection Association, www.nfpa.org/public-education/by-topic/property-type-and-vehicles/school-fires/school-safety-tips.

5. "Why Partnerships Are Important for Schools and Businesses," Partners in Education, www.browardpartners.com/docs/a_importance_pr.pdf.

6. "What Is Site-Based School Management," http://www.teach-nology.com/edleadership/school_goverance/site_based_management/.

7. Cara Ong, "7 Reasons Why Schools Need Strategic Planning," http://blog.envisio.com/7-reasons-schools-need-strategic-planning.

8. "Developing a Vision and a Mission," http://www.ascd.org/publications/books/10742/chapters/developing-a-vision-mission.

Index

alignment: of content standards and assessment, 64; of curriculum and assessment, 63; feedback and, 66; of learning standards with instructional resources, 66; lesson, 40–42; unit plan, 65

analytic rubrics, 25

analyzing (level four of cognitive domain), 31, 32, 33

Application Model, 61

applying (level three of cognitive domain), 31, 32

articulation, in process evaluation, 62

assessment: alignment of content standards and, 64; alignment of curriculum and, 63; classroom, 26–28, 30–31, 65; data, 4, 5; ELA, 27–28; feedback and, 43–44; formal formative, 5, 30–31; formative, 4, 5, 30–31, 33–35, 58, 65; informal formative, 4, 30, 33–35; summative, 5; teacher-generated, 24–28, 30–31; writing, 25

backward design, 29, 30–31

balance, in input evaluation, 61–62

behavior: education as changing patterns of, 54; guidelines, 70

Bernhardt, Victoria, 15–16

Bloom's Taxonomy of Cognitive Domain, 31–33, 36

bullying, 9

business/school partnerships, 77

CCSS. *See* Common Core State Standards

central office personnel, 77, 78

chalk talk, 42

Chapman, Carolyn, 59

checking for understanding, 4, 33–34, 35

checklists, 48

CIPP. *See* Context, Input, Process and Product Evaluation Model

classroom assessments: formal formative, 30–31; summative, 26–28; unit assessment plan and formal, 65

classrooms: culture of, 48–49; management of, 48; as standards driven, 58; student engagement and evaluation of, 45

closed response surveys, 8–9

cognitive domain, 31–33

collaborative planning, 76–77

Common Core State Standards (CCSS), 29

About the Editor

Frank S. Del Favero is associate professor in the Educational Foundations and Leadership department in the College of Education at the University of Louisiana at Lafayette. He holds a certificate of advanced study in educational administration and a PhD specializing in educational administration and policy studies from SUNY Albany. He teaches educational leadership courses at the graduate level involving the use of data to affect change, the evaluation of effective assessments and instructional strategies, and school vision. His approach to teaching at the postsecondary level integrates academic theory with his extensive background as a K–12 education practitioner.

About the Contributors

Nancy P. Autin, PhD, shares her experience in school administration and teaching and her expertise as a nationally certified lead evaluator for school accreditation with aspiring school leaders at the University of Louisiana at Lafayette. In the department of Educational Foundations and Leadership, she teaches courses in vision, leadership, and culture, curriculum planning, and using research for leading change. Her K–12 experience includes principal, academic assistant principal, instructional supervisor, staff development director, mathematics department chair, and teacher. Nancy designed learning opportunities for school leaders focused on promoting a culture of continuous improvement. She provided teacher training in using data to set goals and incorporating formative and summative assessments to bolster student achievement. As vice president and chairman of the board of directors of the Raphael-Evelyn Education Foundation, a nonprofit providing education for Nigeria's youth, Nancy believes the ultimate goal of education is improving life for all mankind.

Tarrah C. Davis holds a BA in elementary education, a MEd in gifted education, a plus-30 degree in education, and an EdD in educational leadership. She is certified to teach elementary grades (1–8), computer literacy, and the academically gifted. Tarrah began her teaching career in K–12 where she worked in both public and private schools for nine years. She has had the opportunity to work in several different teaching environments that have given her the chance to teach in multicultural classrooms as well as multiability environments. In 2011, Tarrah became an instructor for curriculum and instruction for the College of Education. Since 2013, she has worked as the assessment coordinator for the College of Education as well as assistant professor for the department of Educational Foundations and Leadership.

Ronald J. Dore' joined the University of Louisiana at Lafayette as an adjunct instructor in the department of Educational Foundations and Leadership in the College of Education in 2009. He became a full-time instructor in the fall of 2011. Ronald received his baccalaureate degree in French with a minor in Spanish from the University of Southwestern Louisiana, presently known as the University of Louisiana at Lafayette. He received his master's in administration and his specialist degree in supervision from Louisiana State University. He taught English, French, and reading courses in St. Martin Parish for sixteen years. He then became assistant principal for three years and then principal for nineteen years. After serving in the public school system for thirty-eight years, he retired in 2008. As an Educational Foundations and Leadership senior instructor, Ronald is responsible for teaching various topics ranging from the history of American education to the philosophical and sociological foundations of education. His goal is to instill a passion for learning while providing an environment that is meaningful, collaborative, and conducive to learning.

Amanda Shuford Mayeaux is assistant professor in Educational Foundations and Leadership at the University of Louisiana at Lafayette. As an educator for over twenty-five years, she has worked on a variety of campuses spanning grades pre-K–12 in a variety of contexts from teaching to administration. Dr. Mayeaux has won several national teaching awards, including the Milken Educator Award in 2003 and Disney's Outstanding Teacher of the Year Award in 2006, along with her teaching team partners, Monique Wild and Kathryn Edmonds. Her research interests are expert teachers, motivation factors, professional learning, change process, school culture, and effective leadership.

Bertha Myers joined the University of Louisiana at Lafayette as a full-time instructor after thirty-three years in public schools. She began her career in K–12 education teaching at the middle school level and continued as assistant principal and principal of two middle schools, transforming both from junior highs to true middle schools. Myers's focus in interdisciplinary curricula provided opportunities to serve on the administrative team that opened the first true middle school in her district. In 2006 she received the honor of Regional Principal of the Year. Her interests in middle-level education led to an opportunity to develop online professional development modules for Northwestern State University. These modules were used throughout the state of Louisiana to facilitate the training of teachers in the middle school concept. In addition to teaching at the University of Louisiana at Lafayette as a senior instructor, she also works as a consultant for area parishes, where she trains and supports teachers in coteaching strategies in the inclusive classroom.